The Southern Heritage

The Southern Heritage

by
· JAMES McBRIDE DABBS

L. C. Catalog card number 58-9669

© James McBride Dabbs, 1958

FIRST EDITION

TO EDITH
Once Pupil
Long Since Teacher

I have written this book:

For those who love the South so much they want to make it better. For happy, relaxed, confident men, for whom "tomorrow is a day." For farmers, white or black, who in this fruitful land still trust God. For hunters, and for fishermen, who, as Izaak Walton says, are friendly men. For "mannersable" men, who have time to talk. For young men, who want to live. For those who remember our great and tragic past, and for those who do not remember but who are so imbued with that greatness that they face the future with hope. Finally, for all men who, loving their land and their neighbors, love God.

If you find yourself within this list, Reader, read on.

CHAPTERS

The Southern Heritage

CHAPTER I

Southern Heritage

LIKE THE REST of the South, I am confused. Of course, the world is confused. But part of our confusion is rooted in us; if we could see more clearly how we stand within ourselves, the world, including the South, would open more clearly around us. It is hard to see perspectives radiating into the world if we stand off-center within ourselves.

Desiring like everyone else to find such perspectives, and especially to get a clearer view of the road ahead, I review the road I have traveled these sixty years, recalling the actions, scenes, and people that are built into my life, especially those which suggest some clue to my present situation: a Southerner slowed down by racial fog but determined to find a way out.

It would be strange if I were not a Southerner. Sitting by this window, looking down the avenue along which I hurried as a boy and down which I have seen my children and grandchildren walking with their dogs running beside them, I feel the throb of this land in my blood. I was born, in 1896, a mile from here, near the upper edge of the South Carolina coastal plain, in a Black Belt county, of ancestors on both sides who had lived in this state for one hundred and fifty years. At least two of them fought in the Revolution; one of these was murdered by the Tories. It seems to have been the custom of the Tories to "murder" their opponents; the Whigs only "killed" theirs. My father's father fought in the Confederate War. My mother's father did not; he died of consumption during the war. By 1900, however, that war had faded into the past of old soldiers almost as much as the First World War has now faded into mine, and they seldom spoke of it to little boys unless the little boys bothered them too much.

My father's background was farm, my mother's plantation. Upon those productive units rests the history of the South.

My childhood home was a farmhouse of four rooms, and one of its chimneys was clay. But a mile away, down a wooded avenue, stood the plantation home where my mother had grown up and where I'm living now: a house weather-beaten in my boyhood, unpainted since 1860, looming gray among the trees, with tall columns and long halls, bitter cold in winter but deliciously cool on summer days. This was my second home: between farmhouse and plantation dwelling my boyhood swung. Life was no richer at the plantation—we were all land poor—but there was a certain spaciousness there, partly physical, as of broad piazzas and halls, partly spiritual, as of people who, if they wore the cares of life, to a small boy seemed to wear them lightly.

My father did not wear them lightly. Not that he fretted about them, he did something about them. He was a newcomer in the community, and as a landless man who had married land he was on the make. He was a man of the future, a pioneer who, before marriage, had worked in the foundries of Anniston, Alabama, and had thus helped to bring in the New South of Henry Grady. Forced to return home by an attack of typhoid, he spent his energy in new methods of farming, in the development of the Farmers' Union, in farm politics, and in the Prohibition Movement, which sent him to the state legislature in 1906.

For he was a puritan also, and also Southern in this. The puritan strain runs strong in the South, along with the moonlight and magnolias. He didn't talk to us about duty. We did our duty—or else. From him, and from the farm, we learned that life has meaning. What we did belonged to the farm pattern. Perhaps that early conviction is stirring in me now, asking what is the meaning of the South today. I've never been able to admit confusion and be satisfied.

As pioneer and puritan, Father was critical of his conservative neighbors. Many a time I've heard my mother restrain him with the quiet "now, dear." Many a time, also, I've heard him criticizing the sermon before he got out of church. He always slightly disapproved of my mother's people because they were too easygoing. With one or two of them he quarreled; I remember especially a quarrel with my mother's uncle which Father tried to pass on to me and my older brother, then twelve and fourteen respectively. Ironically, we declined it. For we applied to the problem the critical attitude he, perhaps unintentionally, had taught us, and told him politely but firmly that, though we didn't blame him for quarreling with Uncle Jimmie, we didn't feel we should carry the quarrel on. Thus, whether from sheer Southern individualism or from a true Southern sense of the larger family, the kin, or from both, we stood for the kin against Father himself.

When I was ten, my father made the typical American gesture: he pulled up stakes and moved. Only a mile, it's true, and to escape the malarial miasma, not to find wealth. But he left a settled place and deep in the pine woods threw up a shack until he could build a house. We lived in the shack for sixteen months, curtains for inner walls, flooring laid on two-by-fours on the ground, frogs hopping indoors at evening, and sometimes a snake. In summer the thunderstorms marched through the woods, at times with spaced thunderbolts in line with the house, first a mile away, then a half, then perhaps a quarter, and then—and we held our breath—beyond the house this time, and the immediate danger had passed. I helped my father lick that new land, in the Southern tradition of forest into farm.

If my father was farm, my mother was plantation, with the ease which comes from that background. They say I called her "Mother-Lady" when I was tiny; in this, at least, I showed gentle manners. Sometimes I found them hard to learn. It was she who cautioned me to say to the hostess "I've had a nice time" regardless of the misery of the evening; and, though my father's sense of fact sometimes made me gag, I said it.

Father was reaching for the future; Mother, living on acres that had been her family's for a century, was rooted in the past. She did not live in the past: she was too robust for that. She brought the past up to date, thus dignifying the present. She was like the warm light-bread she used to make—until one unfortunate day she sat down on the rising bread and never baked bread again.

After that I had to go to my grandmother's for light-bread; and, I am told, that was my urgent cry as soon as I entered the hall.

My grandmother's household turned more strongly toward the past. The head of the house, my bachelor uncle, was a quiet, humorous man who once remarked in my hearing and to my youthful amazement: "Ideals are a sin; we should love God." He was the true con-servative, so aware of the goodness which surrounded him that he viewed doubtfully any suggestion of change. If he wasted regrets over the past, I never realized it. He seems to me now the embodiment of the manners my mother tried to teach me. During my childhood he was librarian of the church library, and the easy, humor-ous dignity with which he loaned and received books stands in my memory as a thing apart. He did every-thing correctly, but with the faintest smile, as though to say he knew what he was doing and could do it another way if necessary. He was a balance of reserve and open-ness, of formality and informality, which the South aimed at but often failed to attain.

As regards the past, his mother and his aunts who were a part of the household were conscious of faded glamour. It was through them that I gained a nostalgic sense of the Lost Cause. One of these great-aunts—who was, however, only my mother's age—taught me in my earliest school days. No national flag floated over the schoolhouse, nor flag of any kind, but the inner walls were beautiful with the various Confederate banners, and on Friday afternoons we sang "The Bonnie Blue Flag" and "Maryland, My Maryland." I grew up on *Two Lit-tle Confederates;* and once I almost came to blows with my older brother over the question whether we had ever been beaten in war. I said we had, he said we hadn't. With the fighting about to start, I was prudent enough, he being considerably heavier, to inquire what he meant by we? "The United States," he said. "Oh," I said, "I mean the Confederacy." Perhaps he was less purely Confederate than I because he was just old enough to remember the imperialistic Spanish-American War, and the Confederate General Joe Wheeler leading the U.S. cavalry against the Spaniards with the ancient cry: "Give the Yankees hell, boys."

Once when I was about sixteen I heard my grandmother, standing on the piazza just outside this window, say she'd never been reconstructed and she never intended to be. That was the sharpest pro-Southern remark I remember, and it didn't sound especially dangerous, since my grandmother was a rather small, quiet old lady.

Certainly that lost past never drew me from the vital present—or, at least, not for long. It was rather like a poem in which, strangely, my people had taken part, a tale "of old, unhappy, far-off things, And battles long ago." Perhaps because of the combined spirit of my father and mother, I criticized it without condemning it, and loved it without being lost in it.

The Presbyterian church, of classic beauty, a half-century old when I was born, was a part of the past. It was mellow and quiet. Even the sermons were quiet: long, reasoned arguments in theology. But I never realized how safe it was, how little to be disturbed by the puritan fervor of my father, until years later I discovered in the graveyard an inscription that praised a former pastor for his "urbanity."

Standing somewhat between my father's people and my mother's was my father's uncle, a gray-bearded Confederate, who lived with us. An ancient in appearance, he evidently belonged to the past, and, seated in his lap after supper, I had a vague sense of far-off fighting days. But, like my father, he was a pioneer. Visiting with my father the Charleston Exposition in 1902, he being then about eighty, he was so fascinated by the new inventions and their possibilities for a different world that he was moved to exclamation. He said, in effect, that when he saw what was coming he'd like to live twenty-five, fifty, a hundred, five hundred years, until, realizing the absurdity of his wishes, he blurted out: "Why, Gene, when I see everything they're going to invent, I'd like to live to see the whole thing wound up!" An ancient fighter, maybe, but still looking for a fight. The old *joie de vivre*. But there was nothing Parisian or cosmopolitan about his speech; he was a crusty character. Once, trying out my new hatchet, I chopped three chops in an oak near the back gate. When he saw the scars, he said in my hearing that whoever did that "ought to have three chops on his ass." Yet I have seen this same gray-bearded fighter, standing in twilight among the pigs cracking corn about his feet, turn to face the new moon in the clear western sky and sweep off his hat in a stately Spanish bow. Then he jingled silver in his pocket. That, he said with a faintly amused smile, was for good luck.

Though my father was farm and my mother plantation, though he was the future and she the past, their devotion bound them inextricably together. It was a quiet devotion; "dear" was the most affectionate term I ever heard used between them. There were sharp exchanges at times—at least, his words were sharp. We felt the tensions between them. But around the tensions we felt her enveloping calm; and, being told years after her death that only she had been able to calm him in his angriest moods, and that by a hand upon his arm and the one word "Eugene," we did not doubt it. Sensing their differences, we sensed more deeply their love. Standing with him beside her open grave—I being then twelve—I heard him groan: "My God, I killed her!" Though I didn't know then, as I don't know now, just what he meant, I never doubted the love, however tragic, which surrounded my boyhood.

All this means that I would bring to the race problem, when it arose, a fairly complete, and happy, Southern heritage. It did not arise in my boyhood. First, because such an abstract thing as race relations would weigh but lightly upon a boy surrounded by such a family and facing such arduous tasks. Second, because at that time the race problem was pretty well under cover in the South. Though the pot has never ceased to simmer, in my boyhood the bubbling was almost inaudible. The South had just finished disfranchising the Negro through constitutional conventions and statutes, practically all the segregation laws had been written, and the Supreme Court had rendered, the year I was born, the now famous Plessy *v.* Ferguson decision legitimatizing "separate but equal" accommodations. Perhaps my father thought that the race question had been settled for good. I never heard him or my mother speak of it. That labor was a problem, however, is proved by the fact that in 1906 he was one of the South Carolina farmers who tried to use Belgian labor—Dombrey and his wife, Haas, and Meztok—and was not unhappy, I think, to see them leave for Chicago about a year later. I remember wrestling with Negro boys at noon sometimes as we lay in the shade far down by the swamp, and playing with them from time to time. Perhaps I don't remember more of this because we were six children in the family and didn't need extra playmates, and because Father didn't want people about the yard doing nothing. I remember no feeling against Negroes; but that I had the usual sense of white privilege is indicated by one event I have never forgotten. Walking home from school one day, not yet ten, I met the usual crowd of Negro children also going home. I must have been accustomed to the privilege of the path along the edge of the dirt road, for, suddenly, when I came face to face with a Negro girl much larger than I who apparently wasn't going to give way, I drew back and hit her hard in the stomach. A Negro boy objected: "That ain't good business." "Good enough for me," I snorted, and walked on. I wasn't ashamed, but I didn't tell Father or Mother.

Howard Odum has described in *The Way of the South* these relatively calm years about the turn of the century: "In the quiet scenes of a rebuilding South there were few indications of the length and breadth and depth of the struggle that had been the South's, or that was to be the South's. It was as if, from this quiet midstream vantage point, the long and devious ways in the past, now in the way of being forgotten, were to be matched by the long and difficult ways of the future."

For me such difficulties came slowly. I remember nothing about race during my four years at college.

There may have been an idea or two dropped into my mind, but if so they sank so far below the surface as to be completely forgotten. During those summers I attended "Y" conferences at Blue Ridge, North Carolina, conducted by W. D. Weatherford. I know now that even at that time Weatherford was facing the race problem, and it is possible that he spoke of it during those conferences. I remember the fading sunsets beyond the Great Craggies, and the youthful ideals that, despite my uncle's doubt, shone in that fading light; but if these touched the problem of race, I don't remember it.

During a year of graduate study at Clark University, I was aware that there was a Negro student or two on the campus. But this was a strange land, and one might expect strange customs; I had gone there, after some effort and trouble, to study, and they weren't any of my business. My father had taught me to stick to my job. I felt more or less the same when, about two years later, during World War I, at a casual officers' mess in France, I looked up from dinner to see a Negro lieutenant taking his seat opposite me. I realized that this wasn't done in my neck of the woods, but, then, I wasn't in my neck of the woods and, more importantly, I was over there to fight Germans, not to settle protocol on race matters. Toward the end of the next July—it was 1919—I was passing through Washington on my way home. I had read in the papers that there was race rioting in that city, but I had no feeling about the matter at all. I simply stayed at the station between trains. I had crossed and recrossed a wide ocean, and come safely through a year in France, and was now within five hundred miles of the young wife I'd left behind;

and I didn't intend to have a brick fall on my head on Pennsylvania Avenue—not if I could help it. Four years after this, at Columbia University, in a class which had been seated alphabetically, I remarked to the student seated at my right that I was thankful his name was— let's say Daniels. He asked why. Because, I said, if it weren't for him, I'd be seated by the Negro girl Davis on his right.

Ten years after this—1933—my wife died. As a consequence of that disaster, there came to me a realization which had nothing to do with race directly but a lot to do with people. This was the realization that, in my failure and disappointment, I was simply a human being and was experiencing the human destiny.

Also as a result of my wife's death and its apparent injustice, I became interested in the problem of justice. It was this interest, in part, that brought me back to the plantation of my mother's girlhood, which was now mine, and to the responsibility of running that farm— it was no longer a plantation—with some regard for the several tenants who did most of the actual work. The tenants happened that year to be Negroes, but the matter of racial justice hardly entered my mind.

The fact is that, though it's in my mind now nineteen years later, I'm still uncertain just what place it occupies. My first concrete concern with the race issue had nothing to do with justice. It came when Olin Johnston, then governor of South Carolina, having taken note of the Supreme Court decisions in regard to the Negro's voting, called the legislature into session for the purpose of so amending the laws as to ensure the Negro's not voting in the South Carolina primaries. I wrote a letter to the paper. I said, in part, that I was shocked at what the legislature was doing. Not shocked at injustice, but at bad manners. Not shocked that white people should try to hold on to privileges, but that they should be so brazen about it, doing it in the broad light of day, with the press flaunting their actions before Negroes as well as whites. I don't know how they could have done it otherwise, but it seemed to me shockingly bad manners the way they were doing it.

I am not defending my apparent lack of interest in justice. I risk the charge that I seem willing to have bad things done in a good way. I don't think this is true, but I don't understand at the moment just what my reasons are. It may be that my confusion is also the confusion of the South, and that the clarification of my mind may clarify somewhat the mind of the South.

As for segregation, my attitude for years after the legislative incident was largely one of growing weariness. I was my uncle's nephew, only one generation beyond him in our advance into the modern world, and, though I never felt that ideals were a sin, I certainly wasn't going overboard in the 1940's for the ideal of desegregation. I was merely questioning segregation. All institutions are to some degree burdensome, and I, who once had almost sunk beneath the burden of life, who had kept afloat largely through the inborn will to keep struggling—I wanted to know why we did what we did. Having been spiritually shipwrecked, I viewed life with Ortega's "tragic, ruthless glance," concerned to find something to cling to, discarding everything that did not buoy me up. Under that ruthless glance, segregation did not seem to buoy me up.

By and large, the South in 1865 was as lost as I was in 1933. Not only were most white families touched by personal grief, but the social fabric itself was fluttering in the wind. Why, and how, then, did the white South find in segregation a life-preserver? Why does it cling to it still? Is it possible that the shipwreck of the sixties wasn't complete enough to develop a tragic, ruthless glance? I'm sure I don't know. Nor do I know anyone who does. Yet it is questions like these that will explain us to ourselves and so make us more assuredly the men and women we wish to be.

CHAPTER II

A Pause for Reflection

BUT THE WEB is tangled and the unweaving will take time. Let us stretch our feet to the fire and try to untangle it. We are the South. The problem is in ourselves, and, standing as we do today on a moving frontier between a great agrarian past and a great industrial future, we need to understand ourselves, what past we carry within us and what sort of future may find rootage in that past.

I face this problem as I have always faced the problems of my own life. I have never wished to reform myself; the implications are too drastic. I have wished to form myself, to discover the essential spirit of my life, to become in fact what potentially I am. This has been in part the problem of discovering what sort of person he would be who was equally imbued with his mother's acceptance of the past and his father's longing for the future.

I have no desire, then, to reform the South. It would be futile anyway. What I should like to do is to learn what the South is striving to be, as she hesitates now between the past and the future. She once had, by all admissions, a style of life. I should like her to have that again. The only way she can have it is to be what

it is in her to be. And the better she understands her
many impulses, the more effectively will these weave
themselves together and give her a form, a style, a manner of life suitable to the present but reminiscent of the
past—as one of her own girls is beautiful now but reminds us also of her mother. I have no more doubt of
the fire which burns at the heart of the South than I
have of that which burns at my own. Why should I?
They are both the same. If I probe our confusions, then,
it is merely to stir the embers to a blaze and let the
bright flame burn away the dross.

Doubtless many of us, however, while admitting
some general confusion and the need therefore for some
reflection, feel—if we are white—that we aren't confused about the Negro; we can see what's wrong there.
If only he were let alone. Specifically, if only the National Association for the Advancement of Colored
People would let him alone.

Yet today, in the summer of 1957, the Southern
newspapers, and indeed casual conversations, suggest that
more than the NAACP is involved. A South Carolina
paper is happily digging up the sordid details of transient
labor camps in New York state manned by Southern
Negroes, and white Southerners are laughing over the
discomfiture of these Negroes newly arrived in the
North. The effect of this will be to keep Negroes in
the South. Yet a powerful desire among Southern whites
today is that Negroes should go North; there are even
legislative proposals that they be resettled there. What
do we want them to do?

My guess is that we want to keep them here because, quite simply, we like them, especially "in their

place," where we find them highly convenient; but we want them to go away because at the present moment they seem to be getting out of their place and, instead of being helpful, becoming highly inconvenient; but, again, we don't want them to go away because that might suggest they aren't happy in their place, and this notion would make us doubt both our judgment and our goodness.

It looks as if we're confused. If it's any comfort, I think the Negroes are too. They are no disciplined army advancing under the leadership of the NAACP. A Negro preacher whom I have known for decades said to me recently: "You don't know how confused we are. Far more than white people realize, we have always taken outstanding whites as examples. What can we do now when the white leaders are saying such harsh things about us? We can't imitate them." A Negro leader said to me in Savannah, quite simply: "We are deeply confused." Speaking recently at a Negro church in a Southern city where Negroes and whites have been locked in a boycott, I was struck by the mood of the congregation. Perhaps I was deceived, but it seemed to me as if these people were saying to themselves: "God grant that this white man means what he says!" As justifiably suspicious as they were, I felt they would still accept much white leadership if it were offered honestly. They know little better what to think of us than we what to think of them. If both races could realize and admit this, we could confer more graciously and charitably together. It is time for all of us to make the "pause that refreshes" a pause for reflection.

No one doubts that the National Association for

the Advancement of Colored People is one factor making for change, and therefore for some confusion, in race relations. But before concluding that this is the only thorn pricking the South, let's ask a few questions. In recent years has the world let us alone? I mean us whites-and-Negroes-together. What of the global wars, the Cold War, subversive activities, the existence of communism in the world, the rise of China as a great power? What of the freedom of India, and the bubbling caldron of Southeast Asia and Indonesia, and the white man's loss of face in the Far East; and, today, the Suez Canal; and, tomorrow, Panama?

Or what of the rising standard of living, satisfying some old wants and creating many new ones? Or the soaring cost of living, and the recent falling standard among farmers—who are still the bulk of the South? What of the loss of world tobacco and cotton markets, and now the Japanese challenge to Southern textiles? And, going further back, what of the T-Model Ford, and the resulting network of paved roads, the loosening of family ties, the weakening of small communities, and the growth of the cities?

Did all these things happen without changing people? Without changing, therefore, the relations between people? Between whites and Negroes? To ask the question is to answer it. Suppose no NAACP had ever been imagined. Life would not have let the South alone, would not have let the Negroes alone, would not have left race relations unchanged. The white South always hoped this wouldn't be so. We hoped it under slavery; we have hoped it under segregation. We hoped and believed that in both cases we had set up a static order which would continue unchanged. (Yet even now, cursing the NAACP, we also curse plowhands because, still acting, as we have taught them, like plowhands, they run tractors up trees.)

Whatever our dreamed-of Southern society, of slavery or of segregation, might have become if left alone, it was not, it could not be, left alone in the dynamic world in which it was established. It would have been changed whether anyone, inside or outside, ever thought about changing it; it would have been changed by general forces moving in the world. The proof that it couldn't exist by itself, and that the South has been at least vaguely aware of this for a century and a quarter now, lies in the fact that Southerners have been preeminently politicians. We have always been, and still are, the most politically minded part of the nation. Why? Because, more than any other section, we have had the impossible political job of keeping a changeless social order in a changing world. One hundred years ago our greatest statesman, Calhoun, failed at that job. He knew he had failed. Ten years before the guns roared at Sumter he died with the words "the poor South" on his lips. Our politicians don't seem to be succeeding too well right now. They're not to be blamed for it, any more than Calhoun was. We have set them an impossible task: in a changing world, to keep a changeless society.

I recall a typical scene that suggests, and perhaps to some degree explains, the failure of the South to recognize clearly her relation to the world. You turn off U.S. Highway 17 in coastal South Carolina and drive slowly along winding roads, sometimes clay-surfaced, sometimes the old track where in earlier days "the slow wheel poured the sand." You pass by fields and along great unkempt hedges left to break the sea winds, through deep woods sweet with myrtle and open spaces covered only with pines—the "pine-barrens" of the early settlers. The sun shines, the sand spins under the car wheels, slowly you get the sense of being in a strange world. The road turns again and widens out, and there, spread before you on a slight rise, is a great grove of moss-hung live-oaks surrounding a plantation house, and, beyond, shining between the trunks of the trees, the quiet waters of a river.

The men who lived in settings like this—or even faintly resembling this—behind a barrier of woods, in sunny glades on the banks of quiet rivers, had instilled in them the sense of being alone, masters of their own affairs, kings of little kingdoms. Yet the river ran by the doorstep; and from these secluded plantations, from these magic kingdoms, curtained, perhaps, oh so delicately by Spanish moss, and along these quiet rivers, the planters traded with the world. Isolated from the world and apparently independent, they were really bound to it by the periodic arrival and departure of the boat. They became accustomed, therefore, to living their own lives without realizing how dependent they were. The South developed the psychology of a folk society and the needs of an industrial society.

I suggest that we forget our unhappy politicians for a little while, stop trying to persuade anybody, even ourselves, and reflect. We have a tremendous store of goodness around us and within us, far more than we realize. We do ourselves an injustice by defending ourselves so hotly. We merely need to be, for a little while, our more quiet selves and turn the matter over in our minds. We are the people who stand by the fence whittling and, with great good nature, sell or buy a hog or a cow or a blooded horse. We are the people who sit on our piazzas in the evening or on Sunday, or for hours on the bank of the creek watching the float on the quiet water. We are the people who pause on the busy street to pass the time of day, or in our offices push our work aside to chat with a friend, perhaps even a stranger, during business hours. Within this basic quiet lies the power to solve our problems. Recollecting ourselves, we shall face even the race problem with a certain detachment.

It hasn't been long since it was bad form to suggest that there was a race problem. No one brings that up now, though there is still considerable opinion that if we left it alone it would solve itself. Maybe so. But it won't be left alone in the world we live in; and we have to live in that world. Therefore, with our politicians still standing upon the battlements and shouting defiance to the vague hosts they see approaching, it might be well for us to try to determine what we are defending, what we can defend, what we want to defend. Let us avoid the mistake our fathers made in '61. By their own admission—this was certainly true of the leading state, South Carolina—they went to war to defend slavery. Before the four bitter years were done, they were cursing slavery and sometimes, unfortunately, the slaves. Today's battlements are metaphorical; there are no fire-eating Rhetts and Yanceys any more. But the politicians like to imagine themselves in the midst of a struggle, and indeed they are, but, fortunately for them, a bloodless one. While they shout on, then, concerned of course to save not only the South but also their jobs, let us pause for a moment to understand the shouting, and so make the struggle as reasonable and its event as desirable as we can.

CHAPTER III

The Land We Love

THEY SAY they are defending our way of life. What is our way of life? They say segregation. Are we defending segregation as an end or as a means? Considering its nature, one would suppose we are defending it as a means. As social beings we do not normally practice separation, of which segregation is a form, just for itself. Yet I am afraid we have fallen here into a common trap: we are so concerned with the means that we find in it the end. Segregation is basically a means of separation, a fence, and the virtue of a fence is to keep things in or out. Imagine a frontier land where border fences are necessary to keep out predatory animals. Would the promoters of such a land advertise it as a place where men might build fences and live behind them? Who would come to such a land?

We keep up the fence of segregation to protect what we consider the values of our life here. We have built this fence not at the Mason-and-Dixon Line, but most intricately and involvedly across the entire South and through our own hearts. It does not include the South; the South, and Southern hearts, include it. It separates the races in the South. But what unites the races in the South? Geography, of course; but within that geography there exists a common life, with common virtues, developed through three hundred years. I do not at the moment contend or deny that these virtues are equally distributed between whites and Negroes. I only say that they are here, and that they must be the values we are trying to defend.

What, then, are we walling in or walling out? Of course, we didn't build the wall; our fathers did, and they probably knew what they were doing. But we are maintaining it, at considerable material and spiritual expense, and—I speak now both for canny Scotchmen, by whom the South is partly populated, and for lazy Southerners, by whom the South is largely populated—I should like to know what we are really defending.

What is the Southern way of life which men have longed for when absent and fought for when challenged? It's more than hot biscuits. But I'm afraid most of us have only a dim idea of what it is. This isn't surprising. All men live by broad and therefore vague convictions, and we are not exceptions. But at the present moment we are under challenge, and it would therefore seem well, in order to defend ourselves successfully, that we gaze for a little while upon the face of the land we love.

The land and the people. For, though the land helps to shape the people, and though, shaped by it, we love the land itself, what we love most deeply is the kind of people who live here and the kind of life they live. Other regions and countries may show some of the same characteristics we do. We are human beings, and there are certain similarities in the lives of human beings everywhere. But we are Southern because we are more one thing than another. That we are Southern there can be doubt, whatever makes us so. Even if it's only a state of mind—which it isn't—it works, fusing us together and sometimes, unhappily, against the world.

First of all, we love the land. All men love "the hills and valleys of their native land," but how dearly depends upon the degree and nature of their association with it. The South is pre-eminently the place where Southerners live. A friend who has lived in several parts of the country tells me there is one sure mark of the Southerner: his first question is "Where're you from?" If you reply: "Well . . . I hardly know. There was San Francisco, and Omaha, and . . ." his expression changes and you become to him, if anything, a slightly strange being, perhaps interesting because strange, but not one of the folks. But if you're from the South, who knows? With all his family connections, you might be kin to him.

But the South is more than one big family, it is still a farming section, where there is much land and scattered people, and where, because of this, and because land is the farmer's job, one sees more of land than of people. There are also many days to see the land in. Our winters are open; there is scarcely a day when you cannot work or play outdoors. It's a land, therefore, of hunting and fishing, sometimes by whites and Negroes together, especially the boys. Perhaps Negroes have hunted more than whites because they were more often hunting for food; but both races know of dark pools in deep swamps, of old fields where the partridges feed, and of all the numerous margins of cultivation where the crop breaks into the wild. Men tend to love all long-continued associations; this almost universal association with woods and streams in a mood of relaxation binds the South together.

We also love the land because, foot by foot, we have fought across it. The South lost the Civil War partly because she chose (and was forced) to fight it on her own soil; but when time, the master poet, has made poets of us all, the sentimental value of a war lost, especially if lost on native soil, is greater than that of a war won. Though the North includes one great field of the sixties, immortalized for the nation by Pickett's wild charge and Lincoln's quiet words, the South includes a dozen, among them Chancellorsville, the Wilderness, Cold Harbor, Seven Pines, Vicksburg, Shiloh, Chickamauga, and Atlanta. This is the land of our blood; we have made it our own.

By the same token, the North has made it its own too. Much of the South belongs to the heart of the nation. It is hard for the South to admit this, and hard for the North to understand it.

Deep in the past, behind the Civil War, lies the Revolution, which was partly fought, and some say won, in the Southeast. There are swamps in South Carolina, almost unchanged in one and three-quarter centuries, where Marion hoarded his forces and whence, with the help of Sumter and the other partisan leaders, he needled Cornwallis across the northern border and along his unhappy road to Yorktown and the end.

In this land there exists a society where leisure, however it may fail in fact, is still sought as ideal. Maybe we have as much leisure as we did; maybe it's just better distributed. It's true we have a swiftly increasing number of labor-saving machines, and these, though they increase the leisure, have tended to infuse their nature into us, so

that, surrounded by leisure, we are in danger of losing
its sense. The spirit of the South has been just the opposite. In the midst of work we have had the sense of play.
We are the despair of the more energetic Northerner,
who feverishly figures how much more we might do if
only we would get on with it. I suppose we act as we
do because of the climate, our economic system, and, in
the past, hookworm and malaria. The climate discourages
too much work. Its continued fairness also reminds us
there's little need to hurry. "There's more fair days than
foul, Cap'n," said one of my tenants when I urged him
to get on with some work. He probably also realized that
I was urging him to get on with *my* work. For our
economic system has been frankly exploitative, so that
those on top gained leisure from the work of others, and
the others, seeing how attractive it was, got it as best
they could in the interstices of work—or, perhaps,
worked in the interstices of leisure.

There's a curious entry in Mrs. Chesnut's *Diary from
Dixie:* "Grant's dogged stay about Richmond is very dis-
gusting and very depressing to the spirits." Mrs. Chesnut
was naturally depressed by Grant's insistent presence,
but it was peculiarly as a Southerner that she was dis-
gusted by the way he *worked* at war. No play; no style.
Better the thrust and parry of Lee; best of all, the dashing
raids of the cavalier Stuart, sashed and plumed.

Being leisurely, the South is also neighborly, for the
first requirement of neighborliness is time. It can't be
streamlined; it allows for the idiosyncrasies of actual people; wherever life is highly organized, it goes by the
board. The South is neighborly also because it has so
much space; a farming area, in many places a pioneer

area, with people scattered widely, often with woods between and sometimes trackless swamps and precipitous mountains. You can't be neighborly with people if too many of them live too near. You'd never get any work done, for one thing, and the South has always managed to do some work; and for that reason, but also because of the too great conflict of temperaments, you wouldn't want to be neighborly; so you'd organize the community services, and then you wouldn't have to be neighborly. The South still needs to be neighborly and wants to be neighborly.

As an extension of neighborliness, there is a basic friendliness, linked, curiously, with a slight reserve. The friendliness is generally American, related to the generosity of the land. The reserve is Southern. Edward King, a Northerner who traveled over the South about 1875, found the Southerner kindly underneath but standing more upon his dignity than the Northerner or Westerner. Practically the same comment was made recently by a foreign student who had traveled over most of the states. He was received, he said, a little more quickly into Northern and Western homes, but a little more completely into Southern. We have here the Southerner's slightly greater sense of the self-contained person, the product of a highly personal society. The purest example I know is that uncle who was skeptical of ideals but who talked as if he had some happy secret that perhaps you had too.

The South is, or is supposed to be, a hospitable land. I know that visitors have come, even in the old days, and gone away without being properly entertained, but the story has generally been otherwise; and the story was a legend even before the Civil War. Whether or not everybody was hospitable, there were enough people, of sufficient standing, sufficiently hospitable for the South to take this as an ideal. Southerners have been hospitable mainly because nature is generous, and because hospitality is natural in a land of kith and kin. Much of the vaunted hospitality of the antebellum South consisted of dinner parties that were arranged by neighbors for neighboring kinfolk and were a part of the community life.

Closely connected with hospitality is good manners or courtesy. Southern courtesy isn't what it used to be —if it ever was—but it may still be noticed. It is related to our conservative society, our sense of social order, and our productive system. However individualistic the Southerner may be, he is also keenly aware of the community. Probably the best Southern manners exist, as to the white people, among those who have economic security combined with some tradition; as to the Negroes, among the race as a whole: both inner spirit and outward circumstance have combined to produce in them a resilience and an adaptation to the present which is near the heart of good manners.

A land, finally, where every man has his place. This, of course, is a slight overstatement. We aren't quite so happy a family as that. We are, however, happier than we commonly think, and for reasons not commonly realized. The white South has been accustomed to think it was happy because the Negro had a place. It has usually claimed the Negro was also happy because of this; but that it didn't quite believe its claims is indicated by the fact that it spent, and spends, a lot of energy in "keeping the Negro in his place." What the white Southerner really means, when he uses the invidious phrase "I like the Negro in his place," is that he likes the caste system of the South. By implication he likes the white man in his place too; and, as that includes everybody in the South, he likes everybody in his place. In this he is merely human, for nobody likes anybody out of his place. In an industrialized democracy, however, a man's place is so vague and changing it's hard to tell whether he's in it or not. Liking people in their places, we tend, in such a society, to be indifferent to, or to dislike, others except as we know them personally. As a result, social cohesion grows weak; men stand apart like atoms; they do not belong to society.

The South being as yet incompletely industrialized, men do not stand apart like atoms, nor are they flung together like atoms in great industrial combines. The South still maintains a strong trace of its old organic quality. Everybody has some place, even beyond his assured but still questionable status as white or colored. He has a place in a community, among kin-people, in history, and perhaps just as a concrete person. This is true of people everywhere? To a degree. But more true of us here in the South.

Though Ford invaded the South too, puncturing many self-contained communities with arterial highways and drawing off thereby much local blood, Southern communities are still relatively more important than those of the rest of the nation. A man lives among neighbors, and, though they will not forgive him everything, they do not forget his assured status as neighbor. As for kinship, the South is by definition the land of kith and kin. Among a thousand Southerners picked at random, there will be more kin-people than among a thousand other Americans picked the same way. The South has never been flooded with European immigration, nor has its population been generally so mobile. Again, the thousand would claim more kin than a similar thousand elsewhere. Why? Simply because, with its family and feudal tradition, the South thinks kinship more important. A man's place here depends more upon his kin than it does in the North. As for the past, that hardly needs arguing. The South is not only a country with a past; it is almost a country of the past. It has had such an interesting past —delightful, tragic, and outlandish—that what it didn't have it has since imagined. As a consequence, many a Southerner today is descended from great forebears who actually lived, and many another from great forebears who never lived; and it doesn't make much difference which is which. We have created enough ancestral heroes to give every man one—certainly every white man, even many Negroes. Southerners, like all early folk, are descended from the gods. The Golden Age lies behind us.

And then there's a man's place just as a man—the solid, concrete person. I remember the gray-bearded blacksmith of my boyhood, a tough old man with several "wives" of several colors. We accepted him as the symbol of sin and let it go at that. For he was a good blacksmith. Nowadays we grow modern and commercial, and in the cities cultivate personalities for sale. The South as a whole, however, is still frontier enough, individualistic enough, financially foolish enough, still enamored enough of the cult of persons, all the way from the great captains—Lee and Jackson, Jubal Early, Bedford

Forrest, and Jeb Stuart—down to the village drunk, to grant a man a certain status simply because he is a man, especially if he wears that manhood with a flair.

Doubtless this multiple sense of place is a gift more to the white than to the Negro. Nevertheless, Southern Negroes also feel the strong pull of their communities, physical and social, of their kin—from the white point of view, inextricably mixed—and of striking personalities. The past does not mean so much to them as a whole, though there are many Negro families who carry their ancestry proudly back to free Negroes or outstanding servants of slavery times. For most of them, however, the rich ore of that past is as yet unmined. Some few begin to realize that upon the rock of their suffering they can build their lives. Martin Luther King, Jr., of Montgomery, knows this.

Taking the South as a whole, we can see what a physically complex thing the Southerner's sense of place is. It is not an abstraction, the result of political or economic power; such power is important in the South, though not so important as in some places. The Southerner's place is primarily physical. It implies an actual place, a particular community of flesh-and-blood neighbors, many of them his kin, some living and some dead, the latter lying in the graveyard beside the neighborhood church or under the cedars yonder in the field. The Southerner therefore has a place in nature, among men, and in time; and this place, or status, is not essentially a matter of being better or worse than others, however much racial status may have blurred this understanding. The Southerner possesses, deep down, the sense of a fitting and orderly world, a cosmos. It is this sense of a cosmos, of the dovetailing of life into life and of life into nature, that causes even the liberal Southerner, if he have any piety at all—that is, if he's still a Southerner —to hesitate before the prospect of sudden change. Ideals are a sin, he says. Notions. Abstractions.

And this sense of place is largely a gift. A man may take some credit for his personality, but his past, his kin, his community are gifts. This is just like the South. Easygoing and relaxed, so self-satisfied, if you please, that she rewards men just for honoring her with their presence. Is it any wonder that Southerners come back home? If only she could have avoided giving status to race, I can't imagine how happy her history might have been.

The South, then, is a land its people love, a land with a sense of leisure, a neighborly, hospitable, courteous land where every man has a place. (I know this sounds too good to be true, but I stick by it!) All these characteristics possess a common denominator: a sense of relaxation, with an accompanying interest in people. Your typical Southerner isn't quite so tautly strung as your typical Northerner or Westerner. He isn't hurling himself quite so rapidly into the future; he has more time for the passing scenery. He has more time. Having time to be interested in the passing scene, he is interested in people, who are the heart of that scene. The heart; not, as in the great industrial cities, the total scene: a mob, without background and therefore without meaning. The presence of the Negro, with his joy in living and his large acceptance of life, is one of the major reasons why the South is like this. The Southerner tends to accept the world rather than to change it; it is a part of his conservatism.

I know the faults that lie at the extremes of this virtue. On the one side, indolence; on the other, violence. The South at its best is relaxed; at its worst it is either asleep or frenzied. We may drift from physical relaxation to indolence; we may erupt out of mental and moral relaxation into violence. Or we may swing directly from indolence to violence and back again. But there is a relaxation that is the accompaniment of faith, of thought, and of action; this is the quality that the life of the South brushes moment by moment.

Though the elements of Southern life are simple, they are intricately woven together. This is the nature of a folk society; the South, though in process of industrialization, retains many earlier characteristics. In such a society, values change slowly and become entangled with one another; in an industrial society, they are added or subtracted. Because its materials are simple, the folk society may seem simple to the sophisticated observer. These materials, however, are so intertwined that the total life is complex. Though the South looks simple, it is hard to understand, even for those in whom the pattern exists.

It is especially hard to understand now because we are shifting rapidly from agrarianism to industrialism, from one form of livelihood to another, and are therefore, though without intention, modifying our way of life. Our vague realization of this makes us uneasy; we are afraid, and properly, that we are losing something. Finding segregation under attack, we defend it as our life. Is it really? Might we possibly win this battle and lose the war?

If our life is as we have just described it, segregation, however related to that life, isn't the life itself. It is far less attractive than the land that contains it and the people it, somehow, contains. We called it a fence, necessary perhaps but hardly desirable in itself. But we need to remember that social institutions shape the people they contain. The institution of segregation, in sharp contrast to the rest of Southern life, is a constrictive force in a genial society. Many Southerners feel it protects that society. Perhaps so. But it also distorts it. This may be necessary. In order to exist, we may have to maintain this wall even in kindly hearts. But we certainly will not do so unless we have to.

.

CHAPTER IV

A Backward Glance

WHAT IS SEGREGATION, really? It has been with us for some time, and to understand it we must know something of its history. How far back must we go? Segregation was established about seventy-five years ago, and was the direct outcome of Reconstruction. It was not, however, the original form of race relations in the South, but was superimposed upon slavery and inevitably colored by it. What, in general, were race relations under slavery?

They were not primarily race relations; they were labor relations. The first Negroes brought to Virginia, in 1619, were indentured servants, and gained their freedom as soon as their term of service had expired. Indicative of the slightness of racial feeling is the fact that there were some marriages between Negroes and whites. These, however, were generally frowned upon, though whether upon the ground of race or religion is not clear. Such slavery as still existed scatteringly in Europe was of infidels. According to English common law, a Christian could not be enslaved. After some forty years' hesitation on this point, Virginia decided it was financially safe to convert a Negro slave to Christianity.

By this time slavery had been accepted. The chief

reason for it was economic. Virginia, for instance, settled strictly as a great plantation of the London Company, upon the failure of that scheme developed the typical Southern plantation: a farm of some size producing chiefly a staple crop and worked by slave labor. Such large agricultural holdings could not be worked by free men because such men were not available: in a country abounding in free land free men work for themselves. But why not, then, simply family farms? (This was, in fact, the usual Southern pattern.) The answer again is economic, though glossed with an ideal. The Southern colonies had lands where staple crops would flourish; these crops could be produced on a large scale with unskilled labor; Europe was clamoring for such crops. Any man who had money to get labor and the means to keep it, and who would take up land in this new country, could satisfy the needs of Europe and grow wealthy at the same time. The game was played first with tobacco in Virginia, and, later, across the South, with rice, indigo, cotton, hemp, and, finally, in Louisiana, sugar.

Seeking manpower, then, such colonists as were able bought indentured servants and, when these were insufficient, African slaves. The colonists did not think up African slavery; the Portuguese had thought it up two centuries before. For those who needed to justify it, there was the excuse that by this means the heathen might be converted to Christianity. That this was an excuse is evident from the action of the Virginia colonists, who hesitated to let their slaves become Christians lest they thereby become free. The excuse, however, was important. The colonists were much closer to the Middle Ages than we are. They settled the new world "for the

glory of God." It was merely an added glory to settle it
with heathen and make them Christian.

But far less justification was needed for slavery in
the seventeenth century than in the nineteenth. In Europe, serfdom, if not a fact, was still a clear memory,
and the lot of the poor was so hard that men and women
were willing to sell themselves into periods of slavery
—indenture—to get a chance at a new world. Furthermore, the clear statement of the ideals of human equality
still lay a hundred years in the future. It was therefore
easy enough, whenever the colonists thought about slavery, to think of it as an appropriate life for these strange,
uncouth, and by all known standards apparently inferior
people, the Negroes.

The eighteenth century brought the rapid growth
of slavery and of opposition to it. This was the century
of the rights of man, and of the American and French
revolutions. Even before the American Revolution, in
South Carolina, which was then building its economic
and political greatness upon slave labor in the tidewater
rice plantations, Henry Laurens and Christopher Gads-
den were opposed to such labor. The Revolution increased this opposition. Patrick Henry admitted that the
only thing which kept him, and many others, from freeing their slaves was the selfish desire for comfort. Jefferson included in the original draft of the Declaration
of Independence a remonstrance against the King on the
ground that, against man's natural right to freedom and
against the objections of the colonies, he had forced the
English slave trade upon them, but this he deleted "in
compliance to South Carolina and Georgia." The more
conservative Constitution only permitted Congress to

vote on closing the foreign slave trade in 1808. Though Jefferson never freed his own slaves, partly on the ground that he had no right to turn them loose in a society which had no provision for them, partly because of bankruptcy, he was deeply concerned about the injustice of slavery, and troubled for his country when he reflected that God was just.

But with the invention of the cotton gin in 1793 and the coming of cotton as a staple, these liberal attitudes faded. Most men were never deeply concerned about the matter anyhow, and the mere passage of time weakened the Revolutionary fervor. At the same time, cotton, produced mainly by slaves, was sweeping across the South, around islands of pine-barrens from seacoast to mountains, and from the Carolinas to the moving western frontier. Cotton meant slaves, and slaves meant cotton. It can be argued that Eli Whitney caused the Civil War.

The first warning came in 1820 with the Missouri Compromise, which, though a compromise, raised the question of what limits slavery should have in the westward expansion into the Louisiana Purchase. From 1820 to 1860 slavery spread westward while the attack and the defense grew increasingly bitter. Up until about 1820 there had been more abolition societies in the South than in the North; after 1830 they practically disappeared from the South and, under the leadership of Garrison, spread over the North. There can be no doubt that the basic reason the South wanted to keep slavery was its supposed economic value. (Even in the South, however, there was disagreement about this value.) But there were several nineteenth-century arguments by which slavery was justified. Perhaps the nearest to reality was the political: property was guaranteed by the Constitution, and the slaves were property: upon them rested the economy of the South. Another defense was the social: how could the white South exist if all these Negroes, apparently of an inferior race and unprepared for freedom, were set free? Related to this was the philosophical, best stated by Professor Dew in connection with the Virginia debates of 1831–2: as society is held together by the existence of lower and higher orders, slavery makes for a perfect society. The scientific defense mentioned the shape of the Negro's head, and the fact that the suture closes earlier in his skull than in that of the white and therefore, it was argued, constricts his brain.

In the field of religion, the preachers of the South returned to the old theme with a vengeance: it was the South's duty to maintain slavery in order that Christianity might spread; it was the slaves' duty, as the Bible said, to obey their masters. The South was religious then as now, and the leadership of the preachers, even the greatest preachers—James Thornwell, for instance—did more than anything else to cement the section in the defense of slavery. This religious defense, though in part a counterattack against the onslaught of the abolitionists, was more than that: it was also the outgrowth of the revivalism which had blazed up in the South in the Great Revival of 1800, and which throughout the century swept multitudes of whites and Negroes into the Baptist, Methodist, and even Presbyterian churches. This was a humanitarian and democratic movement, and many of its followers were led to an increased "love" for the slave even while the laws were binding him more strictly. Slavery therefore took on a quality of special goodness because it put men in a situation in which they sorely needed love.

Finally, closely related to the religious defense of slavery was the personal. Slavery was patriarchal; the master's relation to the slaves was, at its best, paternalistic. He often said, and sincerely, that they were his larger family. Partly from a sense of responsibility, partly from sincere personal regard, he often refrained, against his economic interest, from parting with them, and in many cases this regard and affection was returned by the slaves. In my own community there lived a plantation-owner who, on principle, never sold a slave. When natural increase made it impossible for his plantation here to support his "people," he bought additional land twenty miles away and divided his time between the two plantations.

The development of such personal relations came about as follows. Slaves were first regarded almost entirely as physical labor, or manpower. On the farms, where there were few, they worked alongside their masters and often ate in adjoining rooms; here they came to occupy almost the position of poorer kin. On the plantations the field Negroes remained chiefly a laboring force to the master and, to a lesser degree, to the overseer; but the stable, yard, house, and personal servants stood on a much higher footing and were often held not only in affection but in regard. In the eastern—that is, the older—slave states the position of these Negroes vis-à-vis the whites continued generally to improve until the Civil War; slavery grew more civilized. The westward migration raised the slave's status in certain situations, but lowered it in general. In a frontier situation the slave had more freedom and responsibility, but he paid for it by being more at the whim of his master, who in a new community was less controlled by public opinion. He also paid, on the great plantations, by being more than ever merely so much manpower, separated from practically all whites, immersed in the cultivation of cotton, rice, and sugar cane. Given time, these frontier farms and plantations would have responded to the human aspects of the master-slave relation, and slavery would have become as civilized there as it had on the plantations of the Atlantic seaboard; but time ran out.

Though instituted by force and with force always available, slavery was maintained mainly not by force but by persuasion. The master was often born into his place, many of the slaves were born into theirs, they had little information of any other place, and so they came not only to accept their place but often also to take pride in it. There were, of course, irritations among them as to the working of the system; there were some who rebelled, in spirit and even in fact, against the system. The folk songs of the Negro, their spirituals and work songs, all make clear the slave's dissatisfaction, his longing for freedom and justice and heavenly rest. Apparently, however, much of his discontent found expression in these songs and left him relatively free to tread without bitterness his narrow road. As a consequence, slavery became a social order, a way of life, not only for the masters but also for the slaves, and as such maintained itself with a minimum exercise of force.

The increasingly stern statutes relating to slavery

enacted between 1830 and 1860 seem to disprove this. These were the reaction of the South to the incitations of the North, and particularly to the Denmark Vesey insurrection in Charleston in 1822 and the Nat Turner insurrection in Virginia in 1831; but individual planters seem to have obeyed them as they saw fit, and generally they saw fit to pay less and less attention to them. One of the strictest laws, passed as a safeguard against conspiracy, forbade teaching slaves to read and write; but many owners either continued to teach favorite slaves or to permit them to be taught. When Edmund Ruffin said on the eve of the Civil War that the Southern planters had no fear of disloyalty among the slaves, he probably spoke for the South; the event seems generally to have sustained him, though not so completely as was once imagined.

There is one other aspect of the situation to be noted: the free Negro. By 1860 there were some 250,000 among 4,000,000 slaves. The white South feared them even more than it feared the larger number of slaves. It had some reason, perhaps, in the Vesey insurrection, for Vesey was a free Negro. But its main reason was that it did not know them. Therefore, it passed all kinds of laws against them, to keep them as near the condition of slavery as possible. If there was, strictly speaking, a race problem prior to the Civil War, this was it.

There was in one other relationship the beginning of a race problem. This was the relationship between the poor whites and the Negroes. The poor whites hated the Negroes because, though slaves, the Negroes stood beside and sometimes above them economically, and because they themselves often had to do menial labor

either directly or indirectly in competition with the Negroes; the Negroes scorned the poor whites because
of their pretensions of superiority. As for the white
farmer with or without slaves, his attitude toward the
Negro was mainly economic. If he had no slaves, he
hoped to buy some; if he had a few, he hoped to buy
many. Though these men were actually in competition
with the plantations, they usually overlooked this in their
eagerness to become plantation-owners themselves.

For these several reasons having to do with the relative position of the races in the South, and also for others,
the white South united in the Civil War. It was defending, first of all, the Southern land, second, the accepted
and even sacred institution of slavery.

In 1865 the South collapsed. For a while nothing
was certain, either in fact or in men's expectations and
desires. The whites were more certain than the Negroes,
for they were chiefly concerned to restore the past, ex-
clusive of slavery, so far as that was possible, while the
Negroes faced a new possibility, freedom, about which
they were almost entirely ignorant. They had some leadership in the free Negroes of antebellum days, but, unfortunately for the South, these Negroes had been kept
in almost as much ignorance of the theory and practice
of freedom as had the slaves.

For the white South the immediate problem was
labor. The race problem was as yet a cloud on the horizon. Thus, the old problem remained, only made more
complex by the freedom of the laborer. Much of the
South was hungry; it was all terribly in debt. What ar-
rangements could be made immediately for producing
food and fiber? The South almost immediately enacted

what have been called the Black Codes. Though these were formally labor and vagrancy codes, they were enacted for the purpose of controlling the Negro. Many white men in the South, indeed many slaveowners, were glad that slavery was gone. Even before the war they had fretted under the system, but had not known what to do about it. Now of necessity they faced the question of what to do with free Negro laborers.

Practically no one saw the Negro as anything but a laborer. That he might also be an American citizen and a voter seemed at most a fearful fantasy. A few men considered this possibility, among them Wade Hampton, and broached the subject in the state conventions held in 1865 and 1866 for the purpose of reorganizing the state governments and bringing the states back into the Union under the rather generous plan offered by Lincoln and adopted by Andrew Johnson. But these were lone voices.

As for the Negroes, they were naturally intoxicated with freedom. Doubtless a few of them continued the routine of life on the plantation, but most of them set out to go somewhere, partly to prove they were free. Often they didn't go far—to the nearest town or Federal camp. But this random movement disorganized still further an already disorganized social order. Their attitude toward their former masters, and indeed toward whites in general, seems to have been a mixture of submissiveness, respect, and affection on the one hand, and disregard, disrespect, and impertinence on the other. In general, the freedman deferred to his former master in all matters except the political. Since the political was new, he deferred in all matters in which he had been accustomed to defer. In attempting to re-create the spirit of the time, we must remember that the etiquette of slavery was exact, and that the slightest deviation might well be an "impertinence."

The essential change accomplished by the Civil War in this regard was the narrowing of the gap between whites and Negroes. From having faced one another as free men and slaves, they now faced one another as free men, two groups still vastly different in power but closer in power than they had been. Emancipation, by putting the Negroes theoretically on a level with the whites, had doubtless made of the earlier labor issue something of a race issue. But it was the events of Reconstruction which thrust the race issue to the front. Congress refused to adopt the mild Presidential plan of reconstruction, and, under the leadership of Northern radicals, instituted the drastic Congressional plan. Thousands of whites were, though for only a few years, disfranchised; all Negroes were, by the Fourteenth and Fifteenth Amendments, enfranchised, and—mainly under the leadership of white men from both North and South, acting from high principles all the way to no principles at all—these Negroes took political control of some Southern states and swung a heavy weight in all.

They may not have done as badly as white Southerners think; they never attacked the institution of property. That there was enormous corruption no one doubts, but, then, there was enormous corruption all over America at the time. This was "The Gilded Age" of Mark Twain and of the Boss Tweed Ring in New York: the age when the rest of the country, freed from both the strain and the peril of the Civil War, was feeling its oats in a wild surge westward and up all the ladders of success. From the white Southerner's point of view, however, the main trouble was not that the Negroes governed badly but that they governed at all.

This attitude was to be expected. Take men accustomed for two hundred years to rule—in regard to their Negro slaves, to rule arbitrarily—defeat them in a long and bitter war, destroy the economic base of their life, establish their former slaves among the ruling class, and you get the piled-up bitterness of Reconstruction. More important now even than getting the Negro back to work was getting him out of his position of dominance, back into a position not only of inferiority but also of subjection. It was now that "white supremacy" became a slogan. The term had been used before the Civil War, but it had no particular point for that time; it could only apply to the future and define an attitude that the whites intended to maintain in whatever future might come. Now, suddenly, the future had arrived, and, under the weight of black supremacy, white supremacy became the rallying cry. The issue became primarily a race issue, and the problem assumed its present form and difficulty.

Reconstruction ended with the elections of 1876; all Federal troops were removed by the spring of 1877. During the Reconstruction struggles the Southern whites had been united in their determination to regain control of the state governments, but they had not been united on the means to that end. There were those, like Wade Hampton of South Carolina, who wanted to persuade the Negroes to support the Democratic candidates; there were others, like Martin Gary, also of South Carolina, who wanted to frighten or force the Negroes into not voting against the Democratic candidates. This was, in general, the age-old white division in the South between the more privileged and the less privileged. The more privileged generally were rather favorable to the Negroes, both because they thought they could control their votes through persuasion and economic pressure, and because they wished to use these votes against the less privileged. The less privileged were more opposed to the Negroes, both because they had owned fewer of them as slaves, and often none of them, and therefore retained little control over them and had little knowledge of and confidence in them, and because in many cases they actively disliked them, both as the pawns of their upper-class white political opponents and also as their own active economic competitors. The two groups had different economical and political stakes, in general and in the Negro. There was only one aim they had in common: white supremacy.

For thirty-odd years after 1876 the relative position of Negroes worsened. This showed itself through segregation and through disfranchisement. Generally speaking, these two movements went side by side, and increased in severity and effectiveness as time passed. There was no official segregation before the Civil War, though habits of life kept Negroes and whites pretty well separated. On the trains, slaves and free Negroes could ride on the white cars, though when slaves were transported by rail in a group they were usually carried on freight cars. After the War, segregation came in only slowly, spottily, usually first by custom, then by statute. After 1890 segregation in schools was established by constitution in seven Southern states, or eight, if Oklahoma, admitted in 1908, be regarded as Southern. Education had, however, been in effect segregated since the war. The Reconstruction constitutions allowed for mixed schools, and two of them, Louisiana's and South Carolina's, required them, but except in a very few instances Negroes and whites never went to school together, each race being willing to go to its own schools. The attitude of the Negroes as to schools was probably rather close to their attitude as to churches: they were willing and sometimes eager to segregate themselves. It must be remembered, however, that in the first post-war chaos there were practically no schools. For many years public schools, though called for by state constitutions, remained largely on paper; and private schools were chiefly those conducted, at first through the Freedmen's Bureau, by the Federal Government and Northern philanthropy, and primarily for Negro children.

For a long time after the close of Reconstruction, Negroes rode on the same cars as whites, attended the same theaters, ate at the same restaurants, and drank at the same bars and soda fountains. As segregation laws began to be enacted, there was opposition from some whites. For instance, the Charleston *News and Courier* objected to a proposed South Carolina segregation law as both unnecessary and burdensome: if you segregated coaches, you'd soon have to segregate waiting-rooms and eating-places, and that would be absurd; there might be some excuse for segregating low-class people from high-class people, but none for segregating Negroes in general from whites in general. The laws were passed, however, and within the first decade of the present century the pattern had crystallized.

Negro disfranchisement was accomplished first, both before and after 1876, by illegal methods, later by legal. The Negroes were so discouraged by the success of the Democrats in the campaigns of 1876, and by the final withdrawal of Federal troops in 1877, that not a great number of them even attempted to vote. Yet the white South, with Reconstruction vividly in mind, made it certain by threats, violence, and fraud that few should try, and that even those who voted might find their votes uncounted. As this was a continuing strain upon both the mind and the morals of the whites, they ended it, or at least reduced it, by skillfully rewriting their constitutions. They thus felt they had won a moral victory, for they could now obtain, under the law, the necessary ends that formerly they had had to obtain beyond the law.

These constitutional conventions at the turn of the century were the last large and dramatic fact directly concerned with interracial relationships. If the revolution of Reconstruction ended in 1876, the counterrevolution of Redemption—as it has been called—ended in 1910 with the last constitutional convention. The present racial attitudes of the whites are mainly the product of those forty years.

The Negroes, however, never agreed to segregation and disfranchisement. Booker T. Washington, the greatest Negro of his generation, did, for purposes of expediency, urge acceptance. But his leadership passed with his death in 1915, and since then Negro leadership generally has urged continuing protest. The white South has not heard this because it did not want to.

Meanwhile, life has gone on, since 1914 with a rush; many forces then powerful have receded, while others then unknown have taken their places. Herein lies a basic weakness of segregation: in a changing world, it was supposed to remain unchanged. There were, it is true, a few white Southerners who looked upon it as a temporary training-school from which in time Negroes would graduate. But the white South took it as a final solution, thus indicating that it did not understand the nature of the world in which it lived and from which it necessarily took some coloring.

As if the Negroes weren't at the bottom about 1900—what with the Plessy *v.* Ferguson decision legalizing segregation—the Spanish-American War and the succeeding campaigns in the Philippines put them there. For those events took away the last chance of national aid. How could the North stand up for the colored race in the South while the South itself was enthusiastically supporting the war in Cuba and aiding the nation in bringing to heel a colored race in the Far East? The Negro would have to settle alone his quarrel with the white South; the rest of the country had something else to do.

In the last fifty years the Negro has pleaded his own cause through action, and the world, unintentionally, has pleaded it for him. Slowly he bought land, became a farmer, and gained some economic power and self-respect. At Hampton and Tuskegee he studied to be a better farmer and worker—artisan and craftsman—though the latter did him little good directly, for he met the white workers closing against him, and indeed industry closing against craftsmanship. He has pleaded his cause also through words. In the famous Atlanta address, delivered before the Atlanta Industrial Exposition in 1895, Booker Washington accepted without question the fact of political, civic, and social inferiority; urged Negroes to make of themselves better workers; and held out to them the hope that as they deserved respect they would receive it from the whites. Partly because that was all they could do, they accepted his leadership. The whites approved enthusiastically.

The second advice the Negro received, and has with increasing unity followed, came from the other great Negro leader of our times, a younger contemporary of Washington, W. E. B. DuBois. Speaking first from the Negro university at Atlanta, later from the North, DuBois urged the Negro to keep his eye on all the rights guaranteed him by the Constitution. He admitted that Washington was in part right: men had to make their living, and the better the living, other things being equal, the better the man. But he urged Negroes never to forget, or to let the world forget, that as American citizens they had certain rights, and that those rights were being denied them. Taking up the fight about 1905, DuBois pointed out that Washington's 1895 plan wasn't working, that apparently Negroes were being driven still deeper down. In 1909 he was instrumental in organizing the National Association for the Advancement of Colored People and was for many years one of its leaders. Somewhat ironically, the NAACP was organized primarily to prevent the extension into the North of the race riots incited in the South by such men as Tillman and Varda-man. After Washington's death, Negroes increasingly accepted the more militant leadership of DuBois.

Because of Washington the Negroes have today a stronger economic life and occupy a more important economic position than they would have without him. Because of DuBois they have developed a political and legal sense and a remarkable power to plead their cause within the framework of American law. But more important than either of these men was the world, revolving larger matters and carrying the South with it.

It was a common opinion, about 1910, among thoughtful Southerners and observant visitors, that race relations were growing steadily worse. Said one of these visitors, an Englishman and a student of race, W. P. Livingstone: "If nothing is done to alleviate existing conditions . . . a catastrophe will ensue which will startle the world." No such catastrophe has ensued. Yet the most important actions involving race relations were carried out not to improve these relations but in response to world conditions. Even before World War I, Negroes had flocked to the cities of the South, themselves the product of a world increasingly industrial, and had thus caused to be raised occasionally the question of man-power for the farms. But with 1914 and the succeeding years this question became in many communities a vital one. For the war stopped immigration to America and called many immigrants back to Europe, and flooded the factories with orders for material and their managers with the need for men. This became even more the case in 1917. Some half-million Negroes went North to fill unskilled jobs, often leaving places on Southern farms unfilled. This same rush took place again in 1922, when there was a renewed industrial spurt in the North accompanied by depression conditions on Southern farms. In the ten years from 1914 to 1924 well over a million Negroes migrated from the South to the North. This resulted in frantic efforts to stop the Negroes from leaving: refusing to sell them tickets, taking them off trains, beating up labor agents—and in more sensible efforts to raise wages and improve working conditions.

　　Like all wars, World War I strained old social relations, and because of its particular nature it raised again in the Negro's mind political ideals. Whatever we really fought for, we said we fought to make the world safe for democracy. On top of that, we drafted more than a million Negroes into the army to fight for democracy; and the fact that we permitted only a few to fight and put most of the others in labor battalions only made more glaring the undemocratic treatment they were receiving. We made a few of them officers, but we segregated them in the making and, later, on active duty (not always, however, as I learned, in casual mess halls). In brief, we glorified our democratic effort, put the Negroes into it, and segregated them in it. We came out of the war into several years of serious race riots, partly caused directly by the war, partly indirectly as the war stimulated production and brought Negroes into relation with whites in new and competitive situations.

　　Though the thirties, with the Depression, hit the Negro harder than the white, throwing him out of his job more quickly and sometimes permanently, the period did one thing for him. Under the government benefits, from the original dole to the latest subsidy, he generally shared, though not always equally, with the white man; he even voted with the white man, really for the first time this century, though on purely economic questions. If he now expects the national government to help him against the states, who in his position wouldn't? There was always the Fifteenth Amendment, and now once again there is "the government," promising this time, not the fool's gold of forty acres and a mule, but the real gold of subsidies and supports and social insurance.

Then came the forties and World War II. We didn't shout this time about democracy—the shouting wars were done—but from the way we talked about Hitler and his treatment of the Jews one might think that democracy had something to do with it. Indeed, we admitted we were the arsenal of democracy. And this time we really drafted the Negroes, shunted them back and forth across the country and over the seven seas, showed them the world with all its strange, unsegregated customs, and still on the whole kept them segregated. As a result, racial troubles and riots—and thousands of rumors without foundation. Again Negroes poured out of the South into other sections of the country for jobs. This movement, together with the residential segregation that ensued in Northern cities, has led to the formation of powerful voting blocs among the Negroes in the North.

With the fifties, and Korea, we hardly tried to segregate. The Negro became a fighting man alongside the white. The event has shown that he satisfies the requirements, and since that war integration has been extended to cover practically all areas of military training. This is a long way from where the Negro stood in the white halcyon days of 1910: the golden age of parity, the period in which the whites were so superior I wasn't even aware of it. Now I have to think about it.

But, as a matter of fact, the whites, even in the South, have been wondering about it for some time. As a whole, of course, they have been mainly concerned to keep the Negro down: how much concerned and how far down varied from person to person and group to group. But there have always been white people who have been concerned to give the Negro a better break: from merely better wages to equal treatment with other people. Even during the 1880's, when the South was busily segregating and disfranchising, a Methodist bishop, Atticus Haygood, of Georgia, made an earnest Christian plea for the Negro as "Our Brother in Black"; and George W. Cable, of Louisiana, argued most clearly, cogently, and dispassionately against segregation and disfranchisement. It was no use. The South was too close to Reconstruction. Haygood was tolerated; Cable moved North. Perhaps their failure discouraged like-minded Southerners. For the next thirty years, except for an occasional and rather tentative voice like that of Walter Hines Page or of John Spencer Bassett, both of North Carolina, there was silence. But the critical year of 1919, with its explosion of race riots, brought concerted speech and action. In that year the Commission on Interracial Co-operation was organized in all the Southern states. How much it actually did to ameliorate the condition of the Negro, no one knows. Certain critical situations were tided over, and, probably through its influence; the white churchwomen of the South threw their effective weight against lynching. At the very least it served as a forum where whites and Negroes could meet and attempt to understand each other. It passed from the scene only because its members and others beyond its ranks came to feel, in 1943, that an organization more inclusive in its program should be formed. This was the Southern Regional Council, a group that has generally tackled interracial problems indirectly by working for greater opportunities for all, especially in the economic field. The Council commands the respect of all people in the South who are both concerned for the good of the region and aware of what is going on.

From one other white source the Negroes have received encouragement, though it is hardly fair to call it a white source: it is more accurately an essential American source. This is the Supreme Court. The 1896 decision of Plessy *v.* Ferguson, with its enunciation of the doctrine of "equal but separate" (together with an 1896 decision of Williams *v.* Mississippi), sanctioned both segregation and disfranchisement. In these decisions the Court merely acknowledged the practice of the South (or, as regards "equal," its theory) and the will of the nation. But in 1915, along with World War I, came the decision outlawing the Grandfather Clauses. In this decision the Supreme Court said, in effect: *We have gone far enough in heaping handicaps upon the Negro; it is time to stop and perhaps back up.* That the Negro was again becoming a factor in American life is also suggested by the fact that this was the first decision won by their young and growing organization, the NAACP. From that time to the present, this association has argued with increasing skill the case for the Negro. In 1917, in a Louisville case, the Court ruled against residential segregation. In 1927, in a Texas case, it ruled that a state could not officially prevent Negroes from voting in the primary election. In 1948, in a South Carolina case, it outlawed the primary as a gentlemen's club and opened it to citizens without distinction of color.

In the field of education the Court has for eighteen years been steadily undermining the "separate but equal" decision of 1896. In the several decisions on this matter the Court has been redefining equality, through the Missouri decision in regard to Gaines of 1938, through the Sipuel decision of 1948, through the Sweatt decision of 1950 and the McLaurin decision of the same year, and finally through the climactic decision of May 17, 1954. In this last decision the Court found that enforced separation in education in itself means inequality.

In the changing attitude of the Supreme Court, therefore, the road runs clear from 1915 to the present, and the direction indicates the increasing importance of the Negro in the United States. Not only in the United States; in the world. Just as our venture into colonialism about 1900 weakened the Negro's position in the United States, so the approaching breakdown of colonialism strengthens the position of the Negro in the United States. The most striking example of the more than Southern significance of the Southern Negro is, of course, the Civil War itself. Though the North did not enter the war to free the Negro, it did enter it because he was enslaved. For a little while, however, in the late nineteenth century, he was largely forgotten; the South's racial problem could be considered in the Southern context. Now, seventy-five years later, it has to be considered not only in the national but also in the world context. This is perhaps the main source of both our difficulty and our irritation.

CHAPTER V

Wilderness Years

THE WHITES AND NEGROES of the South have been related under two systems, slavery and segregation.
We assume that segregation is the better of these.
In what way? In what way, if any, worse? No one, of
course, wishes to go back to slavery. Nobody at all is
crying for the fleshpots of Egypt. If it appears, however,
that in some details segregation was itself a going backward from slavery, we might wish to change those details.

But it may be objected here that, even though such
a comparison might reveal certain present evils which,
as evil, should be eliminated, the South is being asked to
make these changes too fast. The demand, however, is
neither so sudden nor so great as we are inclined to think.
The trouble is, we have failed to recognize the many
small changes that haven't yet found clear means of expression. There's a similarity here to the closing years
of slavery. In the mid-nineteenth century slavery was
changing, usually for the better. There were numerous
men, North and South, who believed that in the not-
distant future the South would end it voluntarily. Meanwhile, however, and casting doubts upon this possibility,
the plantations were moving westward, and some South-

erners, foreseeing the end of further expansion of slavery in the United States, were looking with greedy eyes toward Cuba and Mexico. The North, therefore, both the industrial and the humanitarian North, felt it could not wait, and the pressure against the South rose steadily until it eventuated in war.

So, now, though our institutions are changing, they aren't changing fast enough, in the opinion of some people in the South and of many people outside the South, to protect the nation. Given the years, we might change without outside influence; we might not; but we aren't given the years. Today, time is of the essence. Margaret Mead, the anthropologist, tells in *New Lives for Old* how the Manus in the South Pacific, under the influence of World War II, changed, and successfully, in twenty-five years from the stone age to the air age. It's true we aren't the Manus; we have more strength, more pride, and a more complex culture. Nevertheless, we too live in the world, which is changing, and, willy-nilly, we are changing with it.

As we don't usually advocate segregation as an economic good, in comparing it with slavery we shall consider only the human gains and losses. If the Negro has gained under segregation—and I am sure he has—he has gained chiefly because he has been, in law, a free man. Theoretically, he could at least move freely from place to place and receive the benefits that belong to such mobility. Also, under freedom he has gained some education, and this has aided his rise and strengthened his challenge of inferior status.

But segregation shows certain losses. In the first place, there is a weakening of personal relations. No one will maintain that the master of the household established personal relations with all the slaves on a large plantation; but it is evident that such relations were established between the master class and grooms, yard servants, house servants, and especially personal servants. Also, on the farm where there were only a half-dozen slaves there was a close relationship between whites and Negroes. It is true the relations were always between superiors and inferiors. These distinctions were admitted, however, generally without question. The spirit, therefore, was seldom corroded by the realization that one occupies, and unwillingly, a position in which one does not belong.

Furthermore, these positions carried definite and continuing responsibilities. Without denying the cruelty always possible in slavery and upon occasion evident, one inevitably concludes that, by and large, slavery in the South was humane. And for two reasons. First, economic: the master treated the slave reasonably well because he had invested in him not only his money but also his chance of success. Second, moral: both the master and the slave were human beings, with passions, wills, peculiarities of their own; and, no matter how much each was concerned to use the other in the rather close and continuing relations of slavery, each was modified by the other and considered the other not merely as an object but also as a person.

Under slavery the whites had not been afraid of these personal relations. The basic institution was so firmly fixed in law and custom that within that institution men could develop personal relationships. Under segregation this aspect of the system is radically different.

Slavery grew up naturally, along the frontier of a world that, though it had outgrown it, had not long outgrown it and was still accustomed to the labor system of indenture, itself a limited form of slavery. Though segregation also to some degree grew and was generally legalized after the fact, it appeared in a world that had just overthrown slavery in a catastrophic effort, and was instituted against a group who were both legally citizens of the nation and objects of dislike to the whites because of the unhappy black dominance of Reconstruction. The South legalized segregation against the better judgment of some white Southerners and against the wishes, now ineffective, of the nation at large. On account of the moral conflict, there was an element of harshness involved which had been absent from the more slowly developing and more accepted institution of slavery. Paradoxically, the system milder in its physical characteristics was harsher in its spiritual. Doubtless the Negroes accepted segregation with some good will, partly because they were learning not to trust the whites anyhow and had some interest in staying away from them, but mainly because they were unable to oppose it and, whatever they might think about their alleged inferiority they had to accept an inferior status and could hardly even question the white man's word that it was just. In certain instances segregation seemed intended simply to make the Negro realize that he was below the white. The main difference from slavery was that, because the Negro under freedom was closer to the white in power, more devices were needed to keep him in a lower place, and segregation furnished these devices.

Segregation did not intend to destroy all personal

relations between whites and Negroes. If it had, it would have forbidden miscegenation and the use of personal and household servants. It merely wanted to be sure that all relationships were of the master-servant type. Though segregation weakened greatly the personal relationships existing under slavery, it did not destroy them, and in some places has not destroyed them yet. But reason would tell us, and all the records show, that the close personal relationships possible under an accepted system such as slavery would weaken and tend to disappear as the men and women who had experienced them died. In addition, many plantations broke up, Negroes moved to other sections or to town, or went North. In recent years the drifting apart of the races has been largely accepted, but it was a standing subject of lament at the turn of the century. All visitors to the South were told of it, and all the thoughtful South was concerned about it. For, incomplete as such a relationship was even under the best conditions of slavery, it was a fruitful thing, and neither thoughtful Negroes nor whites were happy in its fading away.

But it faded not merely with the passage of time, and the breaking of close ties, but also with the nature of the relationships segregation set up. As compared with slavery, these were relatively irresponsible. The landlord had invested no capital in the Negro; he had only invested the Negro's present and recent "living." Why, therefore, should he bother too seriously about the Negro's welfare? He often had the law on his side, so that the Negro would be ruined if he left, and might not even be able to leave. Even without the law, the landlord had little to lose: there were other Negroes waiting.

The same applied to the laborer: he drifted from place to place; if he wasn't going to stay, why should he be concerned to please the landlord? Consequently, there was little concern on either side.

Even more serious morally than the relative irresponsibility between the landlord and the laborer is the fact that under segregation power over the Negro was extended to every white man without any accompanying responsibility. Under slavery, as most Negroes were property, a white man had to move with caution against any Negro not his own property lest he fall afoul of the law. Emancipation, however, freed the Negro from his individual owner only to make him in a sense the ward and property of the state, and every white man became an unnamed official of that state who exercised certain rights and privileges over every Negro. As there were no real responsibilities attached to these rights, the effect upon the white people of the South has been most corrupting. For, though I do not agree with Lord Acton that all power corrupts, I do agree that power without responsibility corrupts; and that's the kind of power the whites have held in the South under segregation.

Finally, race relations under slavery tended to improve with time, under segregation to deteriorate. Both slavery and segregation have been means through which whites and Negroes have worked together in a common social order; but slavery tended to emphasize the togetherness, segregation the separateness, as the name of course implies. As a consequence, whites and Negroes are further apart than they were under slavery and even than they were under the early days of segregation; there is more race consciousness than ever. Segregation was instituted to make the Negro realize he was a Negro and belonged to an inferior caste. He has therefore become increasingly aware of his race but also increasingly determined, as a citizen of the United States, not to remain inferior. Therefore, in unofficially segregated urban areas in the North he has become a power bloc. If white people regret this, they have only themselves to blame. To expect to maintain a lower caste in a democracy is to expect the impossible; it will use its very caste structure to attain general social ends.

To point out the weaknesses of segregation as a system of race relations is not necessarily to imply that the men who instituted it might have done better. It is always possible that in a given situation men might have had more light and less heat; but the light and heat attendant upon the founding of segregation appear to have been about what one might expect. It is not our job to praise or blame these men. It is our job to maintain and to create such institutions as express the temper of the present. Is segregation such an institution?

CHAPTER VI

Why, Then, Segregation?

THERE'S A REASON sometimes offered for segregation which, though flimsy, should be mentioned. According to this, we have segregation in order to satisfy a racial instinct: a supposed instinctive sympathy for one's own race as against all others. Only one question is necessary here: if such racial cohesiveness is instinctive, why support it by law? The "instinct" argument is really an argument against segregation. There are indeed race consciousness and racial sympathy, stronger in one situation than in another, but they are products of culture, not of nature, and are affected by custom and law. Those supporters of segregation who claim that racial feeling is instinctive are trying to get the backing of nature or of God; but they indicate a lack of confidence in their own argument by asking for law to support instinct.

There are sounder arguments for segregation. It is a wall, erected by our fears, against certain real or supposed dangers. These are related to the existence among us of a minority group, the Negroes, whose actual or supposed inferiority endangers the white race and the white culture. In order to lessen this danger, the Negroes are segregated. The whites are too, but the rules are applied much more leniently to them, and, further, the action was initiated by them primarily for their protection.

The first fear, that of cultural deterioration through unrestricted contact of whites and Negroes, is superficially reasonable but becomes of doubtful validity when examined. It is based upon a misunderstanding of what Negro culture is both in general and in the South. In its most extreme form it rests upon the assumption that Negro culture is not only something entirely different from the white culture of the South, but also that it is an African, indeed a savage, culture. Is this true?

As we are laymen, we must in fairness turn to students of race. They say that if any African elements remain in the culture of the Southern Negroes—excepting a few sea-island Negroes of South Carolina and Georgia—they are so vague and subjective as to be doubtful of scientific proof. Melville Herskovits, an authority on the history of the Negro, is inclined to believe that there are slight African traits in the importance of the mother in the family, the emphasis upon funeral rites, and the resiliency of character which Negroes seem to possess. The last, however, is a general attitude that might appear in any relationship. Another authority, E. Franklin Frazier, says that Herskovits may be right, but that the points have never been proved, and that the observed facts may be explained without going back to Africa. All students of Negro life point out how slim were the chances that

African cultural details would survive into the modern world. The slaves came from various tribes, spoke various languages, were deliberately separated in the South, forced to learn English, carefully indoctrinated by being placed under older slaves who had accepted the regime, and forbidden to carry on their African practices. Being a pre-literate people with no written language, they had only the slightest chance to remember beyond a lifetime their African experience; and the facts seem to show that they have almost entirely forgotten it.

With the present achievements of Negroes before our eyes, with a steadily rising standard of living among them, and with top-flight Negroes in practically every field, it seems rather late to raise the old question of the implied inferiority of the Negro because of the lack of a modern civilization in Africa. Yet the question is raised and should be answered briefly. First, though Africa has never had an industrial civilization—a Western creation of yesterday—the native Africans of the slaving period, especially those who were brought to America, were not savages but pre-literate folk with a complex agricultural, social, and legal society, with skilled workers in iron and other metals, and with great artists, especially in sculpture and wood-carving. Indeed, the invention of iron-smelting may have been brought to Europe from Africa. Second, we don't know exactly what makes a people develop, though the stimulation of new conditions and new people seems to have a good deal to do with it. Third, earliness or lateness of development means little. Where was the white race when the dark Egyptians were in their glory and the yellow Chinese were already an ancient civilization? Indeed, where were our blond

ancestors when Rome was mistress of the world? Blue
barbarians in the forests of the British Isles and Germany
—yet destined, at the mere touch of Rome, to come
surging into civilization. No informed white man can
afford to cast doubt upon the culture of the Negro in
America on the ground of the supposed lack of culture
of the Negro in Africa. Nor can any informed person
cast doubt upon the culture of the Negro in America
on the ground of its being not an American but an
African culture.

But, we say, it doesn't seem like our culture; it
seems strange and uncouth. Maybe so, but if it isn't an
African culture, it has to be our culture, for we are the
only people from whom the Negroes could have got it.
Man does not create his culture out of whole cloth, a
black man creating a black culture and a white man a
white culture. It is possible that there are some personality differences between races—for instance, in relative emphasis on aesthetic and practical attitudes. If Negroes differ from whites in this regard, we shall find the
cultural traits they took from us slightly modified in the
taking. But this would probably be a subtle change,
hardly noticeable in the general glance which we give
Negro culture and on the basis of which find it strange.
Why do we find it strange?

Partly because we see there what we expect to see:
strangeness and uncouthness. In large areas of Negro
life, however, from the point of view of the cultured
white person, there actually is strangeness and uncouthness. But it's the uncouthness of an underprivileged group
climbing the economic and social ladder and making gar-
ish slips. It's the uncouthness of all people on the make

seen from the point of view of those who have arrived
or are further advanced. It's the uncouthness of yesterday in the light of today. The flamboyance of certain
religious practices among the Negroes is the normal
camp-meeting behavior of the whites of a generation or
two ago.

And only in certain Negro churches and denomina-
tions will you find such behavior. In others you will find
the staidness and dignity of the most sedate white congregation. An old Negro on my place, comparing the
"Amens" of the Baptists with the silence of the Presbyterians, said: "Us Presbyterians don' want no answers."

There's another reason why we find Negro culture
uncouth: we know little about it, and we assume that all
of it is of the style of most of it seventy-five years ago.
As we have segregated the Negroes, we have become increasingly ignorant of them. Not knowing what they
are, we tend to think of them as being the same as in
those fearful days when Reconstruction was succeeded
by segregation. But from being a rather undifferentiated
mass they have developed a class structure, with upper,
middle, and lower classes. This is clearly evident in
Mamba's Daughters, DuBose Heyward's authentic novel
of Negro life in Charleston. Also, the higher the class of
a given Negro, the more he has felt the indignity of segregation, and the more he has deliberately kept himself
separate from us, and therefore unknown by us. Yet, all
the time, the more he has changed, the more he has become like us. For, again, whom else could he copy?
And let us not run away with the word *copy* and say:
*Ah, yes, we knew it, the Negro is nothing but an imita-
tor*. We are all imitators. It is thus that cultures largely

develop. And, besides, if we admit that the Negro copied us, we admit that the culture of the Negro, being simply our culture existing among the Negroes, is no danger to our culture.

Well, in my opinion, it is no danger, except as the culture of any lower class is a danger to the culture of any upper class. But even this is hardly any danger here because the lower class in question is copying our own middle and upper classes and becoming like us as rapidly as we, and circumstances, permit. The situation is really less dangerous to our culture than was the admission into the North during the seventy-five years preceding 1925 of millions of foreign-born immigrants. In Margaret Butcher's recent book, *The Negro in American Culture*, we find the proof that not only has the Negro adopted our culture, he has also helped to create it. Witness Negro folklore and comedy; the spirituals; and jazz, now an American and an international language. It's too late to bother about what a so-called Negro culture, under desegregation, may do to ours; it's been doing it, and happily, for a long time. In this light, the fear that without segregation our culture would be swamped appears without real foundation.

Our next fear is that desegregation of the schools would lower the intellectual and moral standards of the white pupils. I shall not argue that this fear is absolutely groundless, but only that the dangers are far, far less than we imagine, and the other choices too harsh to be adopted.

Exactly what process do we have a right to expect in desegregation? To hear people talk, you'd think the Supreme Court, imitating the old parlor game of turn-over-fruitbasket, had ordered an absolute mixing straight across the board tomorrow morning. The Court didn't order anybody to "integrate" anything; it merely said we should stop separating school children on the basis of race, and even the stopping was to be done with "deliberate speed." It's we who have substituted "mixing" for "stop separating," pressing thus the aching tooth to make it hurt more. But we have at least become aware of the "deliberate speed," especially the deliberate part; left to ourselves, we might overlook for the next seventy-five years the "speed," as we overlooked for the last seventy-five the "equal."

We still have, however, the impression of a dark army of Negro children, like a summer cloud pouring up the west, until we see in imagination the cyclone spout and desert the schoolhouse for the storm cellar before the storm has struck. It's a terrifying picture, but that's all it is. There's no such cloud. There are a good many Negro children in the South—in 1952, about two and a half million to eight million whites—but where in the name of common sense are the motives to whip them into a cloud? We farmers ought to read the signs of the sky better than that.

So far as the South as a whole is concerned, integration will come slowly and scatteringly. The city of Washington, being the seat of the national government, was a special case, as was the city of Baltimore, the metropolis of a border state. These show what can be done in certain situations, not what will be done in general. The whites are certainly not going to make a general push to go to school with the Negroes. Why should the Negroes make a general push to go to school with the whites? To reply that they want to be like the whites even to the extent of just sitting close to them and rubbing off some of the shine is to express merely the ignorance of white pride. My county school board has recently built near me two modern schools, one for whites, the other for Negroes. One of the Negro teachers, when asked if any of the Negro pupils would transfer to the white school if permitted, replied: "You could hardly drive them there. Why would they want to go? They have everything the white school can offer, together with the companionship of children they know."

There is one important reason why the Negro may push into the white schools: that is inequality of treatment. Give him equality of school environment and the right to choose his school without regard to race, and in ninety-nine cases out of a hundred he will choose to attend school with his own race. The one-hundredth case will be that rare person in any society, rarest of all among such conservatives as Southern Negroes, who wishes to try the strange and difficult just because it's strange and difficult. But the ninety and nine—why should they leave their excellent classrooms and teachers, teams and clubs and childhood associates, to sail upon uncharted waters? It's only racial conceit that makes us think they would. Negroes merely want the rights and privileges of American citizens. It happens that at present we have a good many more than they have. But desiring an equal chance with us at success isn't the same as wanting to sit with us in school or church.

We seem to think there is a Negro psychology. Negroes are simply people who, in the South, have been discriminated against in certain ways; and if there is anything strange in their attitude toward us, it is because we have been doing and are doing the discriminating, and they naturally want it to stop.

Negroes made practically no claim to non-segregated schools during Reconstruction. Yet this was the morning after the death of slavery, and they were still close to the whites. What they wanted was an education. Now, after having been pushed, having drifted and pulled away from us for seventy-five years, why should they suddenly clamor for an association they didn't even desire at the very dawn of freedom? Have we shown ourselves such tender friends that they now yearn for our presence? We overlooked the "equal" that Plessy *v.* Ferguson said they should have, and thus caused them and the courts to ponder its absence until now the "separate" has been outlawed. We might have avoided this if we had given them the equal schools we admitted they had a right to and they said they wanted. They now have the right to desegregated schools. What they want is schools, just like other people, and let the law forget race. But to think that *they* will forget it, after we have hammered it into them for seventy-five years, and will rush to mingle the pale faces and the dark, is not to think but to head for the cyclone cellar when an April cloud crosses the sun.

What may be the effect of desegregation upon the intellectual standards of the white schools of the South? By and large, the standards of the Negro schools are lower. But in most situations we shall have only a trickle of Negroes into white schools, and even the few who come will be filtered—perhaps not intentionally, though that occurred in the summer of 1957 in North Carolina, but by circumstances, for they will tend to be those who because of unusual ability wish to try new things. But even if these few are run-of-the-mine, our schools should be able to take care of them without lowering the entire school standard. We take care of white pupils who are handicapped by lack of ability and unfortunate social environment.

But suppose in some communities the worst; suppose schools where desegregation results in a student body almost equally divided between white and Negro children; suppose Washington. (I can't quite suppose that in the Deep South, but suppose.) Well, then, you'd have Washington. Which, by the way, isn't exactly the Washington we've been reading about in most Southern papers. If there is a fair group in this country, it's the Friends. True, they believe in reform, but they're too old at the game to kid themselves as to the facts of the situation; and they have been for years in close touch with the Washington situation through one of their number, Irene Osborne. What do they say—and what does Mr. Corning, the superintendent of schools, back them up in? They say that Washington is having trouble over the lower intellectual standards of the Negro pupils, and that, without additional teachers to help them, these less well prepared children will drag down the standards of the schools. Given the teachers, however, the schools will set up extra remedial classes to care for these pupils. If in the past the Negro schools had been as well provided with such remedial teachers as the white, the shift to integrated schools would have been made without this strain. In brief, desegregation has made Washington aware that it has not been conducting its Negro schools on the same level as its white; and now, because the shoe also pinches the white people, they are going to do something about it.

Those who believe, as perhaps some still do, that Negroes are retarded in their intellectual development just because they are Negroes, naturally hold desegregation to be ill-advised because it proposes to educate together two groups of unequal native ability. The weight of presently acceptable evidence does not sustain this earlier view. During World War I, Negro soldiers tested generally lower than white soldiers; but Northern Negroes tested higher than Southern Negroes, and in many cases higher than Southern whites. Furthermore, that test was repudiated by the very men who gave it. There has recently been an attempt to revivify these and similar findings, but it has been effectively answered by a group of eighteen prominent American social scientists. The present scientific view is that no significant differences have been established between races. It is not that none exists. It is simply that none has been established.

This being the case, perhaps we Southern white people could tell science something, for we know from observation that Negroes have less ability than whites. Just as our fathers knew in '65 that no Negro would work unless forced to and none could direct his life without white supervision. We admit now our fathers were wrong. Well, we might be wrong too. It's easy to go wrong in such a matter. We look around us. We see the Negroes; some of us employ them. There's no doubt they are more poorly equipped than the whites. But, now, having made this probably correct observation, we conclude that nature, or God, made them so. This is a most happy conclusion. For it's perfectly clear that the inferior position of the Negro in the South is due either to God or to us; and as it's doubtful democratic and Christian doctrine for us to admit the responsibility, we are happy to pass it on to God.

Unfortunately for our conclusion, we have our fathers' mistaken opinion of 1865. When we really stop to think, we find we are just where science is. We simply don't know about the Negro's native ability relative to the white's. But we do know that environment and training affect any man's ability, and that the Negro's environment and training have been less fortunate than ours; and we conclude, therefore—or should conclude—that probably he's backward because of these factors.

As to the effect, then, of desegregation upon the intellectual standards of the white schools, the conclusion seems to be that if, because of a large influx of Negro pupils (a doubtful possibility), a lowering should occur, it could be taken care of by an increase in the teaching force.

We come now to the question of the possible lowering of moral standards by desegregation. We mean by morality sexual morality, though doubtless we have some faint reference to honesty, truthfulness, etc. Again, I shall not argue that there is no problem, but only that we vastly overrate it.

We don't come to this problem with clean hands and pure hearts. I don't refer to the whole history of interracial sex relations in this country; I merely mean that sexual morality among whites isn't what it was said to be in the Victorian period. There have been two

Kinsey reports since then. One should be a bit skeptical in these matters. We are always apt to see our own present in terms of a more attractive past, and—in this case—the Negro's present in terms of a less attractive past. Both races have changed: we from the strait-laces of Victorianism—if they were strait—and the Negroes from the excesses of Reconstruction.

But if the whites have become less strict in their sexual morality, that simply makes the matter worse. It would, if at the same time there had not been developing among whites and Negroes an opposition to inter-racial sexual relations and, among the Negroes, pride in race and in many cases the economic and social power to sustain that pride. But all this has been happening, and it tends to counteract the effect of a more casual sexual morality.

The basic question is: is the sexual morality of the Negro less strict than that of the white, and would the placing of the young people of the two races in the same schools have unhappy effects upon the whites? This question must be broken down. What Negroes? What whites? Or, as we cannot answer for individuals, what classes of Negroes, what classes of whites? The majority of Negroes still belong to the lower class, but there are in addition Negro upper and middle classes, and these are continually growing. They approximate in their moral attitudes, including the sexual, the middle and upper classes among the whites. In fact, there are grounds for believing that the Negroes of the upper middle class are even more middle-class than the whites, more insistent upon American standards. This is because they have come to these standards fairly recently, they know that Negroes in general are charged with having lower standards, and they lean over backward to prove the charge false.

Such Negroes are also urged toward American standards of respectability by their own people. Says Hylan Lewis, in *Blackways of Kent:* "Respectability—or conventionally moral behavior—is an expected accompaniment of education or a good or responsible job." It is the attitude of Negroes in general that those among them who indicate by the possession of education or a responsible job that they "are going somewhere—or aspiring to—should act like it"—that is, should be respectable.

When we argue, then, that lower sexual standards exist among Negroes, we are talking about lower-class Negroes. The charge is probably correct. Certainly sex relations are less formal. The proof of this isn't merely the fact that there are proportionately more illegitimate births among this group than among the whites. The number of births is related to the use of contraceptives; the lower-class Negro group is the most ignorant of all. But the use of contraceptives in illegitimate sex relations is also related to the degree of condemnation of illegitimacy: the less the condemnation, the less care in preventing pregnancy. There can be little doubt that among lower-class Negroes illegitimacy does not carry the general disapproval it does among whites of any class. Since illegitimate children are accepted somewhat casually, the same must be true of illegitimate sex relationships.

But even this statement needs modification. We tend

to assume that deviations from our social code indicate license, whereas they may indicate the presence of another code. There is evidence that even lower-class Negroes, while somewhat casual in their acceptance of illegitimate sexual relationships among the unmarried, are rather general in their condemnation of such relationships among the married. The fact that some relationships are different from those of the same nature among us should not blind us to the fact that even these relationships may follow a social standard.

In fairness, we should note also that the sex relationships among lower-class Negroes, whether casual or conventionalized, are not racial but class characteristics. The main proof is the acceptance by upper-class Negroes of the American sexual mores. We are apt to be misled here by a string of assumptions: first, that the American Negro today is the primitive African; second, that primitive people have no sexual code; and, third, that in comparison with civilized man they are oversexed. In regard to the first assumption, we have already seen that the Negro was never able to establish here his African culture. His present culture is almost entirely the American culture of an underprivileged minority group. Among upper-class Negroes it is simply American culture. Without the first assumption, the second and third are immaterial. However, we may comment briefly upon them. There is nothing to prove that the Negroes in Africa, or indeed any other primitive people, have more casual sexual relationships than we do. Marriage may not be monogamic, but sexual relations follow definite patterns. As for primitive people being more highly sexed than civilized people, the weight of present evidence is on the other side; if anything, we are more highly sexed than they.

So far, then, as the sexual mores of lower-class Negroes differ from the general sexual mores of the whites, it is due to their life in America. Granted that the history of a fact does not change the fact, it does change our interpretation of it and our expectation as to its future development. The history of the contemporary sexual mores of the lower-class Negro is related to the history of the Negro family. This was always weak under slavery. Sometimes slaves were officially married, often they were simply told they were married, sometimes they lived together without mention of marriage, and often they had sex relations without any pretense of living together. Morally and religiously the planters were supposed to condemn casual sex relations among the slaves. Doubtless many of them did. Especially were they apt to be careful about favorite house servants. But acting against these restrictive attitudes and measures were two forces: the planter's desire for as many slave children as the health of the mothers would permit, and the sexual impulses of the planter and the male members of his family. The general conclusion is that such sex relationships between whites and Negroes were fairly common. With these facts evident to the slaves, what was it worth for the planter to urge monogamic sexual morality upon them? One other factor weakened the development of a strong family life: the relative importance of the mother as against the father. The father only begot the child; the mother bore it, nursed it, and, with the help of the master, fed and clothed it.

With this loose family structure, the Negro was thrown into freedom and the chaos of Reconstruction. The general effect seems to have been the strengthening of those families which had already gained a certain strength, and the disruption and even destruction of many more. Amid this mass of uprooted Negroes, there moved thousands of white adventurers from the North. Of course some of the Northerners were men of sexual probity, but many were not, and as a result there probably occurred at this time considerable interracial mixing. As time passed, some order began to replace this chaos. Negroes here and there gained economic standing, sometimes economic independence. In proportion as they moved up the economic ladder and the father became an increasingly important part of the family, the family unit tightened and Negroes adopted the sexual mores of the white community. At present the upper-middle-class and upper-class Negroes are possibly the best Americans among us: most concerned to defend and extend American customs and American sexual mores.

If desegregation should endanger the sexual morality of the white pupils, the danger would almost have to come from the lower-class Negroes. As the general pattern of desegregation will for a long time be thin and scattering, which Negroes will probably enter the white schools? Surely the best prepared, and only a few of them. As for the lower class, you would have to drive them in. They are too aware of their handicaps, and too passive in their acceptance of the present situation. But what danger is there from the upper class? As we have shown, none.

But suppose, against probability, a mass entry of

Negro pupils into a white school. What white children will associate with what Negro children? The whites of the upper class will associate, if at all, with the Negroes of the upper class. To think otherwise is to suppose that children will start doing what they've never done before. The white children of the lower class will probably be slow to associate with any Negro children; nor will the Negro children associate with them. These two groups have played too long an unfriendly role opposite each other. As for the fact that there may be Negro pupils of distinctly lower cultural standards than those of certain white pupils, there are inferior white pupils now; and for this reason there are some people who send their children to private schools. But most of us take the view that our children will form intimate associations only with children of similar training, and that the presence in the schoolroom or yard of children of distinctly different training will not affect them materially.

Our fear of desegregation is based partly upon the assumption that the Negro children in an integrated school will try to force themselves upon the white children. There again our pride deceives us. On the contrary, many Negroes will sacrifice material benefits to avoid too close association with whites. They have pride: they learned it from us. And the women among them have learned, and the girls therefore will learn, that the approach of white men and boys had better be scrutinized with considerable suspicion.

As to the moral implications of desegregation in the Washington schools, one should speak with caution. First, it is doubtful whether the lessons of Washington mean much to Southern communities; second, it is more doubt-

ful what these lessons are. It all depends upon who reads
them. The Davis subcommittee of the House of Rep-
resentatives held hearings in September and October
1956 and came to conclusions highly critical of the conduct and moral atmosphere of the desegregated Washington schools. This committee was composed of three
Southern Democrats and three Republicans, two of
whom were non-Southern if Maryland be so designated.
These two men refused to sign the majority report and
submitted observations critical of both the conduct and
the findings of the committee. Also in disagreement—in
sharp disagreement—with the committee's report are the
conclusions of two high officials of the Washington
school system, Dr. Carl Hansen, assistant superintendent
in charge of senior high schools, and Dr. Hobart M.
Corning, superintendent of schools. In regard to the
question at issue here, Dr. Corning says: "The school
authorities have no evidence of irregular behavior involving white and colored students together."

Time will sift these contradictory opinions. Meanwhile, it seems unwise to gulp down the supposed lessons of Washington.

If we consider all these things, it does not seem
that such a desegregation of schools as we may expect
in the near future should endanger materially the moral
standards of the white children. I will not say there is
no danger; only that it is slight, that we have grossly
overestimated it, and that, by so doing, we have made it
impossible to balance, like sensible men and women, what
danger there may be against the dangers that may result from attempts at continued segregation.

The final danger against which we maintain the wall

of segregation is called "social equality"; this is supposed to lead to racial amalgamation, referred to among the vulgar as "mongrelization."

What is "social equality," this *bête noire*, this ultimate danger to our way of life? The term carries a vague, horrendous character. All whites are supposed to be against it, they become excited at the mention of it, and yet it is certain that very few have ever tried to determine just what it means. This makes us a little suspicious as we come to examine it.

The general thesis of proponents of social inequality is that Negroes are not and cannot be the social equals of whites. This is a curious dictum for democratic America, where it is generally held that a man is free to move into the class for which he is suited. His social position depends finally upon his possessing certain values; it is his economic position that in the long run is the most important factor in making these values possible. Social inequality is a fact in any society, but in a democratic society it isn't generally singled out as a virtue. In the South, however, one form of it is: social inequality between whites and Negroes.

In spite of all its complexities, this is at bottom a bar against Negroes and whites eating together and sleeping together in wedlock. Out of wedlock, only white women and Negro men are covered; there's an open field for white men and Negro women. Put this way, it sounds both shocking and silly. It's strange that people have to have laws about eating and sleeping together. These are usually considered personal and private actions, performed when agreed upon by the parties involved. It's true that sleeping together may result in children, and if such results of a given union are sure to be bad, then society is justified in forbidding the union. It is upon the unproved assumption that such results are bad that the South forbids interracial marriages. That the South does not deeply believe its own assumption is indicated by the fact that historically it has often overlooked and in the old days even encouraged the having of mulatto children: they became the choice servants of antebellum days and appear extensively among persons of prominence today.

But social inequality extends beyond private eating and sleeping together. It also bars the civil right of using without discrimination public buildings, conveyances, and certain public services. The one most in the limelight now is education. If you inquire the reason for a bar in this more public area, you will be told that if it is let down, Negroes and whites will soon be sleeping together, and so we are back where we were in the last paragraph.

Perhaps a brief history of the social-equality taboo will make it clearer. During antebellum days, when "Negro" was almost synonymous with "slave," the white man's fear of the Negro as a social competitor hardly existed. Freedom was so highly valued, especially by the poorer whites who had little else, that it created a social gulf between all whites and all Negroes. The poorer the white, however, the narrower the gulf and the greater his insistence upon it. Speaking of racial mixing—not, of course, intermarriage—in antebellum Mississippi, Vernon L. Wharton says that "In general, the small farmers and poor whites were strongly opposed to the easy-going tolerance displayed by the planting and professional groups toward such relationships." These non-slaveholders supported secession in Mississippi because, they said, the freeing of the slaves would mean social equality and intermarriage. D. R. Hundley, writing of the South during the 1850's, reports a similar comment from a farmer: "Would you be pleased to see four millions of inferior blacks suddenly raised from a position of vassalage, and placed upon an equality with yourselves? Made the sharers of your toil, the equals and associates of your wives and children?"

Apparently the same general reaction continued after the Civil War, with the lower-class whites as usual more insistent upon the social gap. Wharton says that in Mississippi, during Reconstruction, when a mulatto member of the legislature married a white woman, "Although leading citizens of the community held Smith to be a good man and refused to be aroused over the matter, lower classes among the whites created a great deal of disturbance."

But emancipation narrowed the gap between all Negroes and all whites, and Reconstruction for a time put many Negroes in positions of superior wealth and power. The old ruling white class had been largely ruined. With social equality more than ever a fact, the cry of no social equality became more than ever a slogan. The feeling was intensified by the fact that political power, including political leadership, was passing from the hands of a relatively small aristocratic class into the hands of the mass of whites, and many of these, in their uncertain new positions, needed the prestige to be gained from keeping the Negro socially inferior.

The fear of social equality today is both a carry-over from the truly fearful days of Reconstruction and the natural attitude of men unsure of their position and inadequate to life. Any white man can strengthen his confidence by telling himself that no Negro is his social equal.

Racial mixing was at its height in antebellum days, yet there was little concern then about social equality. This was to be expected: the master race always uses the women of the subject race. Racial mixing was very high during Reconstruction; this time there was great concern about social equality. It is now at a minimum, but still there is concern about social equality. Social inequality is maintained, then, not to keep the races from mixing but to keep them from marrying.

What are we to make of the claim, then, that social inequality is a necessary defense against the "mongrelization" of the race? Merely that it's good rhetoric. In the present climate of opinion, it's much more impressive to say that we are doing something to save the race, especially if we believe in addition that God told us to save the race, than to say that we are doing it to protect our superior status and privileges. We fool even ourselves. Having defined "Negro" as one who has any Negro blood in his veins, we leave the whites purely white. Thus, by definition, we keep the white race pure. Though the colored race may now be mixed to a fareyou-well, that doesn't affect us so long as, through social inequality, the pure whites hold the controlling status. But if now we bring God in, we make him the protector, not of racial purity, but of our racial status. That's pretty shaky.

Nevertheless, there may be those who sincerely believe that social equality, in the larger sense of equal civil and political rights, will lead to intermarriage and so to the deterioration and final collapse of the white race and white civilization. To such people I can say only that their fears seem generally unjustifiable. As to intermarriage, it is doubtless true that as the Negroes in the South come to possess the same rights, civil and political, as the whites, and, instead of being a lower caste, become American citizens like the rest of us, the ban against intermarriage will be lifted, as it is now in a good many states. Marriage is a personal matter, and a democracy cannot justify preventing the marriage of two citizens on the ground of race—especially our democracy, which has in its Constitution deliberately outlawed race as a mark of citizenship. If and when the demand for interracial marriage becomes strong enough, the courts will permit it. The situation is exactly the same as with segregation. Thirty years ago at an old Southern university, Virginia, it was frankly admitted that segregation was essentially unconstitutional and would fall when challenged. Of course, if it could be proved that cross-breeding did damage the race and thereby weaken the citizenry, laws against intermarriage could stand indefinitely, and indeed the present laws permitting intermarriage would be declared unconstitutional. But that has not yet been proved, present scientific opinion leaning, if anything, in the other direction: supposing both parents healthy, any damage from cross-breeding results not from the cross-breeding itself but from the social atmosphere in which the cross-breed develops. If this is one of disapproval, the child will be handicapped; if it is neutral or approving, he will grow up with chances the same as, or even better than, those of pure-bred children.

But, someone may say, history shows that all cross-breed races have destroyed the civilizations in which they became important. There's no way to prove this contention except by such a loose use of the terms "race," "nation," and "civilization" as, given Toynbee's space, to make the proof of anything possible. For my part, I think there's nothing in it.

Where are we, then? Social equality, if by that one means the common possession of the rights of the citizen, may very well in the long run bring the removal of the legal ban against intermarriage; interbreeding has not produced bad citizens, nor is there any proof that it will destroy our civilization. Nevertheless, one may still prefer on aesthetic grounds a pure race, white or Negro, and such a person might wish to prevent racial mixing. (Though to make aesthetic preference the basis for law seems a doubtful procedure.) The question remains, then, whether the legalization of intermarriage would speed up or slow down the rate of racial mixing. I doubt if the statistics are sufficient to be conclusive. If we look at those states where intermarriage is permitted, we find the rate very low and possibly showing a tendency to get lower. This was the opinion of Ray Stannard Baker in 1908. More recent scholarly studies all show the extremely low percentage of such unions. The Reverend Clayton Powell, pastor of a large Negro church in New York City, has just commented publicly (September 1957) that in twenty-seven years of performing marriages at the rate of one hundred a year his own church has married only four interracial couples. When we consider the fact that the sense of race is much more pervasive and intense in the South than in the North, it seems evident that, were interracial marriage legal in the South, its occurrence would be proportionately even less than in the North—that is, almost infinitesimal.

The best we can do in this doubtful matter is to draw reasonable conclusions. The removal of the ban on intermarriage would increase the self-respect of the Negro race. Anything that does this decreases the amount of illicit mixing. But would this decrease of illicit mixing be matched or overcome by an increase of legal mixing through marriage? Knowing how we pick our mates, according to class and cultural background even in a supposedly classless society, I don't see how anyone could argue that there would be much tendency for whites and Negroes to intermarry. Though the right to marry may be individual, marriage itself is a highly social affair, and very few people are so foolish as to marry without some consideration of the effect upon their single and joint careers. When the effect is so tremendous as would be that of an interracial marriage in the South—supposing such marriage legal—not two in a hundred thousand would attempt it. Lovers aren't entirely mad; nor do we fall in love purely at random; we consciously put ourselves in the situation where the lightning may strike. If even while in love people show some glimmerings of common sense, it behooves us to show some as we consider the problem.

But suppose, after all these considerations, we are still fearful about social equality, and sexual equality, and the future of the race. And perhaps some of us are. For this vague notion of social equality certainly carries an emotional charge. People grow red in the face over the thought of what may possibly happen to some descendant of theirs fifty, or a hundred, or five hundred years from now. Something which, though we ourselves may find it aesthetically distasteful, cannot be proved bad. When such emotions attach to such slight, vague, and fairly neutral possibilities, there is something more than meets the eye. The emotion is irrational. It is as if my wife should rush in to me as I sit typing here by the open window on this summer night and, thrusting a rifle into my hands, pour out such words as "Don't you know it's terribly dangerous sitting by an open window like this? Why, a lion may be loose out there in the woods, and any minute he may plunge through the screen!" Well, of course, that's a possibility, and I have more than an aesthetic preference for not being eaten by a lion, but the chances of disaster are so very very slight that I think I might be justified in pushing the rifle gently away and going on with the typing—on the grounds that, though there was one chance in a million of her being right, it was awkward typing with a .38 rifle in my lap, and that if she wished she could sit beside me and protect me.

Why are we so fearful of this shadowy lion we have largely conjured up? I think we are afraid of fear itself, of the fear within us, of our own mistreated and violated selves—in brief, of ourselves. I am no psychologist, but all my experience tells me that when people do wrong they pay for it, and sometimes in most insidious and conflicting ways. Now, no white Southerner, calmly and in good conscience, can sit down and defend the whole course of the white man's relation to the Negro. Granted that what we did was what might be expected in the situations in which we found ourselves; granted that we were right many times; it remains that we were terribly wrong much of the time, and much of the time we knew it at the time, not merely in retrospect. Outside of slavery itself, the loose sex relations of white men and Negro women have been our most grievous fault; but even this was not outside of slavery but the inevitable accompaniment of slavery. And this has always been condemned by the conscience of the South, less strongly at one time, more at another. The white man's mistreatment and rather widespread possession of Negro women, combined with his determination as the ruling caste to keep his own women for himself, eventuates in two hundred years, especially under the conditions of a freedom however theoretical for Negroes, in an abnormal fear in regard to white women. Fortunately, as Negroes rise in their standard of living and in self-respect, and as our respect for them inevitably grows greater, we are both less tempted and less able to commit the wrongs of the past against them, and therefore less forced to feelings of guilt and fear in regard to them.

If we consider all these things, I think we shall be less inclined to bring God into it and justify by reference to his supposed will segregation, racial equality, and racial purity. Our fathers justified the unequal relation of master and slave on religious grounds; we feel sure that, though they may have been sincere, they were mistaken. Are we sure that we are right when we justify in similar fashion our position of superiority to the same race?

At this point someone may object that we are justifying by the supposed will of God our position, not of superiority, but only of white and Negro separation. God made the races separate, and it is sinful to mix them. Even if we grant the premise, that doesn't automatically justify segregation and social inequality. It justifies them only in so far as they serve to keep the races apart. But we know that the white and Negro races in America mingled most rapidly under slavery, and only less rapidly under segregation, and that the more the Negro advances in self-respect—which depends partly upon the respect of the whites—the less racial mixing may be expected to occur. Granting for the moment that God wills the races to remain separate, we should then have to conclude that we were right in abolishing slavery and are now right in ridding ourselves of segregation and social inequality.

As to the premise that God wills the races to remain separate, and even segregated, there are two ways to support or refute it. The first will be used by those who believe that the Bible is a book, not only of religion, but also of history and science, and that we need not go beyond it to determine the right course for our lives. The second will be used by those who believe that we have to bring to the religious ideals set forth in the Bible all the pertinent facts of science and history which we have available.

Under the first method, the classic passage used in defense of segregation and of white superiority is Genesis ix, 18–29; and the classic defense rests upon a careless reading of the passage. The defense is that God cursed Ham and said his descendants should be slaves, and—so it is argued—that these descendants were Negroes. The facts are that it was Noah who, after a drunken spree, cursed Ham and who said that Ham's descendants should be slaves; but not even Noah even implied that his own son Ham's descendants would be Negroes.

Avoiding this fabulous rendering, more thoughtful Biblical readers argue for racial separation from certain Biblical instances of separation, either of individuals or of groups. I rely here chiefly upon Donald C. Miller's criticism of this point of view in *The Presbyterian Outlook* of March 14, 1955. It is true that Cain was sent away and wandered into the land of Nod, but this had nothing to do with race. True that demoralization resulted when the "sons of God" married the "daughters of men," but again there is no proof that these groups represented races. True that Abraham was called to separate himself, but religiously, not racially. True that Jesus never attacked racial separation, but neither did he attack slavery, and yet his Gospel has effectively banished slavery from the Christian world. Finally—and on the other side now—it is true that Peter, commanded by God, broke the stern separative laws of his time and ate with Gentiles.

But suppose we take the Bible, not as a book of secular history nor of science, but primarily as an account of man's relation to God and his attempt to relate his life to the will of God. We should assume from the beginning, then, what apparently we have just proved from the Bible itself: that race is not a matter of religious significance, except as our attitude toward it affects our relations to God and man. What races are is to be determined through historical and scientific study; and how they are best related will follow from what they are.

Races have apparently come into being through the chance mutation of genes; through isolation by mountains and especially seas; through possibly the direct effect, and almost certainly the indirect effect, of climate in fostering one mutation and destroying another; and through mixing with other races. Always when they have met they have mixed. The physical mixing itself has apparently had nothing to do with the rise and fall of civilizations, though the conditions in which it occurred and the attitude toward it have been important. As to there being any pure races, that is nonsense. In brief, for the long run, races don't matter. For the short run, because of contemporary and local conditions, they may matter. For the short run, anybody knows what the race situation will be in the South: two races as we have them now. I can't imagine any sober and thoughtful Southern white man worrying about that today: his sister's not going to marry a Negro. And if, ten generations from now, a descendant of his wishes to, not only will it make no difference to him, but, what is of far greater importance, it will make no difference to the descendant.

What Booker T. Washington said about racial amalgamation is truer now than then: "I do not believe that the Negro is yet willing to disappear. Now that he is beginning to understand his own possibilities, to believe that he has an independent mission in the world, and to

gain that sort of self-respect which comes with the consciousness of that mission, the disposition and the willingness to surrender his racial identity and to detach himself from the life and destiny of his own people are, I
am convinced, steadily decreasing."

Behind the admitted fears we have just discussed
there is another, generally not admitted even to ourselves both because it's the kind of fear no man wishes
to admit, and because such an admission would put us
in a bad light. This is the fear that, given the chance,
Negroes will retaliate. The Negroes in the South today
are the descendants of those we kept in slavery for
some two centuries. But slavery is long gone. True.
And if, since emancipation, we had been deeply concerned to make up to the Negro for the injustice suffered under slavery, or if only we had been trying to
be just, we wouldn't be wondering now whether the
removal of the bars of segregation would lead to some
retaliatory action against us.

This much we can say: that we inflict fewer
wrongs now than at any time in the past. For many
reasons, one of them our own changing attitudes, we
now treat the Negro with more justice than ever before.
Nevertheless, the good we do today does not immediately erase from the minds of those we have injured
the evil we did yesterday. A whole social order is not
re-created in a moment.

It is not as if we had no sense of wronging the Negro and he had no sense of being wronged by us. Always in our more honest moments we have known that
something was wrong; always in his more thoughtful
moments he has known that we were wronging him.

We have let ourselves be misled by his silence into thinking everything was all right. Now, under a barrage of criticism, we tend to grow angry; but the anger is that of a man forced after long denial to face honestly the wrongs he has committed. If we could have wronged the Negro in comparative innocence, as perhaps the Greeks wronged their slaves, and if he could have suffered in like innocence, we might right the situation now without any fear of retaliation. But we are in a sense Christian. We know we have done wrong, and we fear retaliation.

Well, I'm firmly convinced we can forget all about it. As little as we know ourselves, we know ourselves better in this regard than we know the Negroes. Has there ever been any cry from the Negroes of "black supremacy"? Maybe, during the darkest days of Reconstruction, a few faint cries, but that situation is gone forever. Today only an occasional madman among them wants any more than the equal rights belonging to any American citizen. I have known them for sixty years: from playmates, through hoe-hands and plow-hands, to university presidents. I think I could count on the fingers of my two hands the words of bitterness I have heard from them. On the contrary, I have been impressed, year in and year out, by their moderation, their humor, their intelligence. As for bitterness among them, Dr. Charles S. Johnson, until his recent death president of Fisk University, asks why there should be. They have right on their side, and they are winning. The best word to describe the attitude of the Negro today, says Dr. Johnson, is "forbearance." Forgetting, therefore, the past, the white people of the South may drop the barrier of segregation in confidence that the Negro will not take advantage of them.

But, you say, this is unrealistic. One doesn't do wrong for centuries and not pay for it. We have paid, and the Negroes, though relatively innocent, have paid too, since the evil coil began. We are paying now, partly in the fear we're talking about. Men pay for the wrongs committed—though not, as Kipling thought, one by one, but all together. There are plenty of charges, some already collected, some still to be paid, without our assuming that the Negroes, if given an equal status with ourselves, would add arbitrarily to them. If that's all we're keeping segregation for, we might as well let it go.

CHAPTER VII

The Pay-off

WHY, THEN, if segregation does not defend us, do we defend it? Either because we do not understand the situation and imagine dangers where none exists, or because segregation does yield some gain of which we are not aware or which we don't frankly admit to ourselves. Is there such a gain?

I think there is. It consists of certain economic and prestige advantages.

It goes against the grain for us to admit this. In the American democratic and competitive air it is assumed that men have equal opportunities, and that economic and prestige gains go to those who show the skill and the effort to command them. Indeed, the recognition of our actions as motivated by selfish interests is so unusual that many of us are prone to deny immediately such motivation. It is for this reason especially that we need to go back to the beginnings of segregation and racial discrimination and ask why these practices were instituted. We shall be less biased in the earlier situation.

The prestige of race goes back almost to Southern beginnings. The society that grew up in the South was partly feudalistic. Instead, however, of having many ranks, it had in reality two: white freemen and Negro slaves. (Within the white group there was a fluid classification, running from great landowners to poor whites.) Each of the two main groups held by birth its unchanging place. To be white was to be on top, to be black, on the bottom. The whites formed an aristocracy existing upon the foundation of Negro slavery.

As in any such stratified society, each group, with probably some exceptions among the Negroes, accepted its place without complaint. This was the way things were. The slaveowners, of course, kept up a steady pressure to persuade new slaves and the slave children that this was the unchanging order. They also directed toward the entire white group, especially the poor whites, a more vague but still general persuasion to keep alive in the minds of the whites the fact that, though there were economic and other distinctions among them, they were all bound together in the brotherhood of race.

I seem to contradict here what I have said earlier about race feeling being unimportant under slavery. The statement, however, remains relatively true. Though some race feeling existed, it wasn't nearly so strong as it was to become after emancipation. There was no real challenge to the bi-racial social order, and therefore little racial feeling on the part of those who maintained that order.

As we approach the crisis of the Civil War, however, with its final challenge, we find an increasing defense of the social order. Indeed, the pull of the order was so great as to warp even Protestantism, the dominant religion, to its support. Protestantism is essentially a dynamic, individualistic religion. This emphasis, however, is modified somewhat among the Calvinistic sects by a sense of man's predestined place, a feeling that could attach itself to the support of the *status quo*, the continuation of every man in the place he already held, and of course the continuation of the Negroes in slavery. Before the war came, the ministers of the South had become so enamored of the threatened social order as to have forgotten their dynamic individualism and to have adopted the Calvinistic idea of a divinely appointed social order. In this order the white man held the position of prestige.

The war, in destroying slavery, destroyed the status society of the south and substituted for it, at least theoretically, a free, dynamic, "placeless" society. Actually, however, the white South was determined that the Negro still had a place, still at the bottom. Segregation and disfranchisement were instituted to accomplish this purpose. It was claimed that segregation was to prevent race friction, and disfranchisement to maintain the sanctity of the ballot; but, though we may make some allowance for these claims, we needn't make much: the detailed and extensive application of the laws does not support them. What, then, were the real reasons?

It is evident that the chief desire among the whites of the South immediately following the Civil War was to put the Negro back in his place as a worker. There is nothing strange about this desire; it was the natural effect of those hard times. A few whites possessed enough vision to advocate that Negroes be given the ballot. The general opinion unhesitatingly turned down this proposal, yet, I think, without bitterness; the time for bitterness hadn't come. The white South was insecure, and fearful as to what action the North might take against it, especially through the recently freed Negroes; and much of this fear, and of the resultant animosity, was directed toward the Negroes. Near the beginning of Reconstruction, however, in 1868, the South Carolina Democratic convention appealed to Negroes not to set themselves against the whites: you have everything to lose "if you invoke that prejudice of race, which, since the world was made, has ever driven the weaker tribe to the wall."

Among the poorer white farmers and the white craftsmen, however, there may have been racial bitterness from the beginning of Reconstruction. Under slavery the only thing which distinguished the "poor whites," so-called, from the slaves was that the former had the prestige of being white and free. Now they had only the prestige of being white, and doubtless they clung more fiercely to it. The white farmers and craftsmen now came into direct competition with Negro craftsmen, and it would have been strange if they had not desired to maintain a privileged economic position.

But by 1876 and the end of Reconstruction the bitterness of the whites had been greatly deepened and extended. They set to work with a vengeance to put the Negro back in his place. Throughout the next thirty-odd years, through custom, segregation laws, and disfranchisement, the Negro was reduced to a place of economic and personal subserviency. The South was trying to reconstruct within the framework of a free nation as much of the slave system as possible. But emancipation and Reconstruction had not only shattered the system; they had weakened the Negro's acceptance of inferiority relative to the whites. Having tasted, though briefly, the fruits of an equalitarian society, he found it impossible to accept the theory and fact of his inferiority. Mr. Lincoln had said he was free, Congress had said he was free and equal, the Constitution had repeated this, the Freedmen's Bureau and the Union League, with the help of the army, had said maybe he was superior. The white South had said, finally, all that wasn't so, he was still inferior, and that was that.

But too much had been said on the other side. This is the primary reason why the Southern white is far more concerned under segregation than he was under slavery to preserve his superior place: his right to this place is being continually challenged by the Negroes, rising as they are by the forces released within them by such freedom as they have, and on the tide of world democracy.

What makes the post-Reconstruction period especially hard to understand is the fact that two revolutions were occurring simultaneously: the counterrevolution of Redemption, by which the whites put the Negro back in his place, and the revolt of the underprivileged whites of the South against their political and economic masters, a revolt that reached its climax during the Populist movement of the nineties. The whites were not only opposing one another; they were also at one moment opposing the Negro, at another using him as an ally in their struggle with one another. Finally, this three-sided struggle took place during a period when the farming economy of the South, under repeated depressions, was apparently going to pieces.

The general demand for white supremacy indicates

that the white South sought racial prestige. It would be natural, however, if this desire varied in intensity among different groups of whites. With the Negro safely under political control—there was never any real danger of his dominating the South after 1876—upper-class whites, unless just risen to that position, could hardly have been deeply and personally concerned about white prestige. Lower-class whites, however, being much closer to the economic and social status of the Negro, would be far more deeply concerned. As the rulers of the South— the aristocratic landed remnant and the newly arrived farmer-merchants, bankers, and industrialists—were engaged in a conflict with the lower-class whites for economic and political privileges, it would be perfectly natural for them to agree, however tacitly, in the demand of these whites for assured racial prestige.

That the desire for racial prestige was not so strong, however, as the desire for economic privilege is suggested by the fact that during the Populist revolt both sides sacrificed racial prestige for the purpose either of holding or of obtaining economic and political privilege. The Populists, especially in Georgia, drew together the poorer whites and the Negroes in the revolt against the old Democrats; the old Democrats unhesitatingly used the Negro vote of the big plantations to defeat the Populists. Each side charged the other with using the Negroes as pawns and thus going back on the white man's unwritten bargain. Both sides were willing to forgo, at least temporarily, the prestige of a purely white ballot for themselves, one side to maintain certain privileges, the other to gain them.

But to show that upon occasion both white groups

in the South were willing to sacrifice white prestige in order to gain or maintain economic and political privilege vis-à-vis each other does not in itself prove that the whites generally sought to maintain economic privilege vis-à-vis the Negroes. Yet, living in a society where prestige is closely linked to economic status and having held for some two hundred years the economic privileges of free men over slaves, it would indeed have been strange if they had not tried to maintain these privileges. The Black Codes indicate that they did; events since then substantiate the conclusion. During Reconstruction a Georgia Negro legislator was told by the Ku Klux Klan that he was making too much money; they didn't allow any "nigger" to rise that way. Simkins and Woody, writing of this period in South Carolina, say: "The prominent citizens of Spartanburg were of the opinion that a primary motive for Klan activity was the desire of the lower class whites to remove the Negro as a competitor in labor, and especially in the renting of land." At about the same time, white landlords in this state were sharply opposing the Liberian movement because of the "prospect of losing cheap colored labor." A little later, in 1878, the managing editor of the *Springfield Republican,* in a report on South Carolina, said that he found much improvement among the Negroes, and that "the universal testimony of employers is that they have never had so little trouble *with their hands* since the war as during the past years" (italics mine).

During the eighties and nineties such incidents and comments continue. The Negroes were being bound more closely to the soil by the various lien laws; the poorer whites shared this oppression with them. Tom

Watson, Georgia leader of the Populists, saw this, and said to both whites and Negroes: "You are kept apart that you may be separately fleeced of your earnings. You are made to hate each other because upon that hatred is rested the keystone of the arch of financial despotism which enslaves you both." In South Carolina one newspaper argued against the use of Negro labor in the new cotton mills because it would lower the wages of the whites. In Greenwood County, in the same state, there was a general terrorization of Negroes in 1899: "The objective of the ["white caps"] activities was reported to be the encouragement of Negro emigration so that whites could secure at low rent the lands occupied by Negro tenants." Of this period E. Franklin Frazier says: "Slogans concerning white supremacy and equal rights which men used in political contests concealed the struggle for control over railroads, mining rights, and state subsidies. In this struggle the welfare of poor whites as well as that of Negroes was subordinated and the way was prepared for the triumph of the Bourbons."

Francis Simkins, in his *History of the South*, says that this period saw the establishment of one principle of Southern economy: "no position that a white person wanted and could fill as well as a black man or woman was denied to him. . . . In practical respects, then, the Negro was worse off in 1890 than he had been in 1860."

During the 1920's this principle took organizational form in Georgia in the Black Shirts: no Negro is entitled to any job any white man wants. During the 1930's Negroes were swept out of jobs first and remained out longest, often permanently.

The forties and World War II gave many indications

that desire for economic privilege was a powerful factor in race feeling. Governor Dixon of Alabama refused to sign a contract with the Defense Supplies Corporation because of a clause that might bring about "the situation where white employees will have to work under Negroes." In 1946 the South was unanimous in its opposition to the Fair Employment Practices Commission because of the benefits that might come to Negroes under such a law. In regard to the Southern farm situation in the forties, Simkins says: "Southern landlords, angered by the increased wages their black tenants were able to command, turned them off the land, allowed tenants' cabins to decay, and adopted a type of land use that required the minimum man power." The forties also witnessed the creation, wholly within the minds of the whites, of the Eleanor Clubs, spitefully named for Eleanor Roosevelt. These were chimerical organizations of Negro housemaids and cooks. The motivation behind this fantasy lay in the fact that, under a war economy, servants were beginning to demand higher wages—indeed, to demand wages. Formerly they had been "given" two dollars a week and "something to carry home."

In William A. Percy's *Lanterns on the Levee* there are striking illustrations of the economic motive entangled with the paternalistic. Percy honored his father, I should think rightly, as a shining example of the kindly Southern aristocrat. When the elder Percy died, an ex-slave and hunting companion said in tears: "The roof is gone from over my head and the floor from under my feet. I am out in the dark and the cold alone. I want to go where he is." Yet in 1927, at the height of a flood, when

7,500 Negroes were crowded upon the levee at Greenville, poorly sheltered, the rain continuing and an epidemic possible, this same kindly aristocrat used his influence to keep them from being taken off by boat to Vicksburg, on the ground that such a step would endanger Greenville's labor supply. The sun came out, the Negroes lived, the labor supply was saved; and the economic motive behind segregation found one more illustration.

This motive appears from time to time in statements made since the Supreme Court decision of May 17, 1954. For instance, in the speech of Representative J. S. Williams of the Mississippi legislature before the White Citizens Councils rally in Selma, Alabama, November 29,1954. The purpose of the citizens committee of Mississippi, Mr. Williams said, "is to give a direct answer to the National Association of Colored People. . . . The NAACP's motto is 'The Negro shall be free by 1963'— and shall we accept that? We can't have it, for if we do, it would ruin the economic system of the South."

This scattering list of incidents and comments, from 1865 to the present, bears out the belief commonly held by students that in race relations the economic motive is extremely important. It was basic in the setting up of segregation and disfranchisement, it is basic in their continuance.

Likewise, the desire for racial prestige, present throughout our history, is still a factor in racial discrimination. It is a common opinion in the South, dating from antebellum days, that the poorer whites, because of their closeness to the Negroes, are the most concerned of all groups to maintain this prestige. Generally, the intensity of a man's desire for place or status depends upon how much he is concerned to improve that place or maintain it. If he accepts his place, and if it isn't under attack, he is little concerned about it. Now, in our society the more ambitious people—the less satisfied, that is—belong to the middle class. (It should be said, parenthetically, that today even the lower class tends to belong to the middle class.) Among lower-class white people, then, whose position and livelihood are not presently being challenged by the Negroes, it is possible to find both a moderate consciousness of race and a real friendliness toward Negro neighbors. On the contrary, among middle-class white people one may find the most intense racial feeling. Such people are often on the make; they are straining to hold or to improve their position, not so much in relation to the Negroes as in relation to other whites; Negroes call them "strainers" or "half-strainers." Being set against everyone, they are set especially against the Negroes, against whom, as a minority group, it is permissible to be prejudiced.

But what of the upper-class whites? The general opinion is that, being as a rule most secure in their place, and that a high one, they are least concerned to improve or defend it and therefore least apt to uphold against the Negroes the prestige of being white. Yet it is a fact that the present opposition to desegregation often comes from well-placed, secure white people. How explain this?

First, being well-placed, they tend to be suspicious of all change. Second, they often profit from racial discrimination. Third, they are the accepted leaders of their community. Though they may be so far above most

Negroes as to have no pride of place in regard to them, they do have pride in the place they hold as community leaders. But the main job of the white community, as white, is to keep itself distinguished from the Negro community. Therefore, the main job of these white leaders is to keep unchanged the old distinguishing marks, to stand still racially and see that everybody stands with them.

When the conservative South of Wade Hampton and L. Q. C. Lamar was smothered by the radical South of "Pitchfork Ben" Tillman and James K. Vardaman, the leaders of this radical South, whose spiritual descendants for the most part lead today, accepted the job of keeping the Negro in his place. It is the acceptance of this social obligation which, even today, causes many well-fixed, secure white Southerners to act in interracial matters like the bitter sort of whites, though as a matter of fact they have little racial animosity.

Indeed, it is possible that the poorer whites of the South have been charged with a degree of racial animosity which they do not really feel. It is customary for middle- and upper-class whites, when faced with the need for racial readjustment, to say: "We have no great objection ourselves, but the poorer whites wouldn't stand for it: there'd be violence." The part about violence is always said publicly—just as it's being said publicly by Governor Faubus of Arkansas today—so that the lower-class whites know what is expected of them. It is true they have grounds for bitterness, but not primarily against the Negroes. The entire economy of the South rests upon low wages; low wages rest upon racial segregation and discrimination: the Negro sets the wage scale of the South. The white employers of the South often exploit both white and Negro employees, playing them against each other. (This does not deny the fact that the employing South itself is exploited by the North and East.) The whites therefore have grounds for bitterness. It is not permissible, however, to vent this bitterness against the people above them—indeed, as the people above them belong to the white brotherhood, the poorer whites are generally prevented even from realizing the real source of their bitterness—while it is permissible to vent it against the Negroes. The Negroes, therefore, become the scapegoat of a general frustration.

There are many hints of good feeling and neighborliness between poorer whites and Negroes who live side by side. I know a Negro woman who, during the thirties, was employed by the government to alleviate distress among farm families. She reports that the helpfulness and friendliness between white and Negro families was notable—so long as upper-class whites were absent. If any of these appeared, both whites and Negroes played their proper roles. This is what one would expect. Neighbors tend to be neighborly. It takes an effort on their part, or on the part of someone else, to make them otherwise. I am suggesting here that the middle- and upper-class whites, exploiting the poorer whites, have given them grounds for bitterness and have exercised upon them sufficient influence to turn that bitterness against the Negroes. I am suggesting also that the political and economic leaders of the South are generally aware of this situation and justify it on the ground that it is for the best interest of society.

In this view, the underprivileged whites of the South are playing, with whatever confusion of assigned role and native desire, the racial role set them. When Southern leaders say that they would like to improve the condition of the Negro but are prevented by the probable violence of the poorer whites, we have a beautiful case of passing the buck. They have written the lines for violence, and could write other lines if they wished. Not that the poorer whites would learn the new lines immediately. Habit alone is a powerful influence. But they would learn, given a little time and the proper suggestions and, of course, fairer treatment from above.

The power of these leaders to set the role of the masses is suggested by a news item that appeared in the summer of 1957 in the *Washington Star*. Reporter William Hines quoted a Winston-Salem, North Carolina, business leader as follows: "Among us we represent probably 95 per cent of the financial resources of Forsyth County. We quietly passed the word that trouble here would be bad for business and we weren't going to have any. We have this thing so well locked up that a cab driver couldn't get a gasoline credit card without our say-so. No, there isn't going to be any trouble." When limited school integration occurred in September, there wasn't any trouble.

But if the underprivileged whites are playing the role set for them, what of their political and economic leaders? Is their role simply that of conservative leaders of a conservative community who almost automatically carry out their function of keeping the Negro in his place? There is more to it than this. As they have often said—for instance, the Committee of Fifty-Two in South Carolina—they are trying to stop what they consider a disastrous drift toward centralized government, and they see in desegregation an instance of this drift. They are opposed to centralized government, first for traditional reasons. Finding itself a minority section, the South has usually supported states' rights as the best means of defending its interests. There is, of course, an abstract defense of states' rights, but the South has also had plenty of concrete reasons to defend them, and has usually been aware of this. Calhoun's brilliant theory was motivated by his devotion to the Southern situation. The South opposed states' rights when that seemed profitable, as in its bitter condemnation of certain Northern states which refused, on the ground of states' rights, to return fugitive slaves.

The other main reason why Southern leaders—at least, Southern political leaders—tend to oppose the drift toward centralized government is that their positions of leadership are jeopardized by such a drift. Seeing their political and economic power slipping away toward Washington, they are naturally disturbed, and will struggle to maintain this power, partly as politicians but also simply as human beings concerned to hold on to what they have.

But these politicians aren't playing the race issue merely as an instance of the states'-rights issue. The race issue is central to their existence, for it keeps the South solid and they are the politicians of the Solid South. If it should be resolved, the political forces of the South would realign themselves with the political forces of the nation, eyes alert to economic and other interests. Low-income groups, white and Negro, would tend to align themselves with similar groups elsewhere, high-income groups to do likewise. This would destroy the livelihood of the typical Southern politician. He would have to become nationally cognizant and intelligent, and he might starve before he could do so. The race issue is to him, then, the central issue; should that be resolved, he would find himself, like Othello, with occupation gone. He may have forgotten most of his race prejudice, but he knows very well, deep down, which side his political bread is buttered on.

He's playing the same game the Northern radicals played during Reconstruction. They were clearly aware of the fact that their continued supremacy in the North depended upon their ability to foment racial discord in the South, against the mollifying efforts of true conservatives such as Hampton and Lamar. So, today, the typical Southern politician, conservative in appearance but a Reconstruction radical at heart, keeps the race issue alive not really to maintain white supremacy but to maintain his supremacy at the expense of anybody who's so dumb as to be fleeced.

What shall we say of this attempt to use the race issue as a means to states' rights? First, that it's ineffective, even to some degree self-defeating. Here's a rundown on the game. The South, with whatever justification, tried in '61 to break the Union. She succeeded only in strengthening what she fought against. After the war the country did not return to the *status quo*. The original federal government had been destroyed. As early as 1861 the astute British observer "Bull Run" Russell, considering the possibility of Northern success, said: "but success must destroy the Union as it has been constituted in times past. A strong government must be the logical consequence of victory." This is what happened. In the place of the former federal government arose a national government, the product of both reasonable fears for the safety of the union and unreasonable desires for profit and vengeance. The Fourteenth and Fifteenth Amendments are the main charter of this government. The white South has always objected to these amendments, partly on the ground that they were force bills. One may ask seriously: so what? The South had appealed to force. When it lost this appeal, it had to pay the penalty, not only of military defeat, but also of political reprisals. These may have been unwise, but this is the way of war: you never return to the *status quo ante bellum*. The particular centralization of government which Southern leaders are fighting against at present was effected, and indirectly by the South, ninety years ago. We are that far behind the times; we should have taken up arms again in '67. Of course, it was too late then; it's ninety years too late now. The Fourteenth and Fifteenth Amendments have been a part of the Constitution for that length of time and, however adopted, are built into the conscience of the nation. True, the judges are just getting around to pinpointing their meaning, but the meaning has been there for any man to read, and as time has turned the pages the meaning has become increasingly clear, and this is it: the South lost the Civil War.

As a conservative society in a dynamic, even revolutionary, world, the South usually fights its battles too late. Often the effort merely strengthens the opposition. Fighting the NAACP, we increase the powers of that organization. Fighting the national influence upon education and toying with the idea of private schools, we are in effect asking for national schools. And so on.

The second comment upon the politicians' present use of the race issue is that it is of doubtful morality. Even to say one is fighting against civil rights is to put oneself, in our climate of opinion, in an awkward position. The only reason we fail to see this is that, without any regard for present actualities, we equate civil rights with carpetbag rule. That's understandable to Southerners, but not to many others, and yet we cry that we're misunderstood. I should think we've grown somewhat in eighty years; we should be our age; we should accept the society of our contemporaries.

If, through the years, we had been trying to treat the Negroes as first-class citizens, we could now with some grace demand state control of civil rights and civil responsibilities. But we have left them, and kept them, second-class citizens. And now to stand up and shout that we are defending civil rights and states' rights when, as our history proves, our fundamental motive for this defense is that we may act irresponsibly in regard to human rights is not merely to put ourselves in an awkward position; it is to put ourselves in a morally untenable position. Politicians may not be too much concerned about this, but, as our own prophets have warned us, God is.

If, as this chapter has suggested, we maintain segregation in part to maintain economic and status benefits, how much justification is there for this action? The only justification we can offer is necessity: that our lives cannot be maintained without these benefits. This is the justification, such as it is, for establishing segregation. During the last quarter of the nineteenth century, life in the South was a bitter struggle, both to make ends meet and to bring some order into the social scene. The South may not have done the best it could have, but in the light of those days what it did has some justification.

But what justification have we? Economically we are in better condition than ever. Though the standard of living remains lower here than elsewhere, it is higher than ever before. There are still many poor people, but the desperate poverty of the 1890's is gone. As for the need to defend white prestige against the Negro, to hold the Negro in a position of inferiority just for the satisfaction of holding him there, there is no real need any longer. What we feel is merely a vague memory of the (perhaps) real need of 1876. We cannot in good conscience defend it.

Upper-class whites, generally secure in their economic and social positions, have less justification than any other group for their race prejudice and discriminations. Because of their training, they understand better than other groups just what they are doing; in the democratic air of our time, to understand that we are maintaining racial discrimination in order to profit from it is to condemn it. Again, when upper-class whites condone the outspoken prejudice of lower-class whites, they are abdicating the very position of leadership which they feel they are supporting by such acquiescence. As leaders of society, they should be able to see that at long last their society is changing and that it's their job to lead it. The leaders of the Old South were not afraid to stand upon their own feet. The leaders of the New might do well to be more truly traditional than they are.

Yet, though the South is changing, no Southerner would want it to change completely; that would be to lose its identity. The fact that we are mistaken in defending, at this late date, status based upon race should not blind us to the fact that we are defending, however mistakenly, a human value, the sense of place itself. All of us in the South, white and colored, have some place distinct from the racial, and are, however faintly, aware of it: we are all Southerners, we live in communities, have kin-people, a past, and, if we insist upon it, personalities. This sense of place, the product of our past, is being rubbed out by our growing industrialism. Here is where the danger lies. Here is where we should build our defenses.

CHAPTER ·VIII·

The Sacred Pattern

Is IT POSSIBLE that we defend segregation not only for
what it does but also for what it is? Do we really
find some value in it? Our reference to it as "a way
of life" suggests that we at least think we do.

Segregation does have some value, first, simply as a
customary action. All societies find stability in such
actions. A society such as ours, where folk attitudes have
been only partly displaced by industrial, is especially
prone to follow custom. Things are done long after the
reasons for doing them are forgotten. In fact, such a
society, being largely unselfconscious, is always very
vague as to the reasons for its actions. What matters is
that people do the same things over and over.

This Southern emphasis upon custom is partly the
result of our plantation economy. Ulrich B. Phillips
quotes John B. Lamar, of Georgia, as follows: "I have
found that it is unprofitable to undertake anything on
a plantation out of the regular routine. If I had a little
place off to myself, and my business would admit of it,
I should delight in agricultural experiments." Phillips
comments as follows: "In his reliance upon staple routine, as in every other characteristic, Lamar rings true to
the planter type." Clement Eaton enlarges upon this view:

"The conservative philosophy of the planters pervaded nearly every department of Southern life, creating a political theory, a set of economic principles, and a profoundly conservative religion."

There are many white Southerners who maintain certain of the minutiae of segregation solely because it is done. I'm such a person myself. Riding along our neighborhood road, I meet an old Negro, an elder in his church, respected in the community. I nod and wave to him. But there's a lack of complete freedom in the gesture. A moment later I meet a white man for whom I do not feel the respect I feel for the Negro. Yet the wave of my hand is free and relaxed. Does my slightly formal greeting to the Negro indicate I'm prejudiced against him? I think not. It indicates I am still under the influence of the old etiquette of bowing, which I have modified but not dispensed with. Do I, then, lack the courage of my convictions? Maybe so, maybe not. For I am convinced that my job is to live both with this Negro and with the entire community. I know that he is as worthy of a free and equal greeting as any man, but I also know that the custom of the community is worthy of some consideration. The first conviction is related to justice, the second to manners—which, being a general way of acting, can never be entirely just. My gesture brings the manners slightly more in line with justice, but not enough to shock either the individual or the community. Too great and sudden familiarity would displease even the Negro. It's been a long time now since I could exclaim: *Let justice be done though the heavens fall!* If that principle had been invoked from the beginning, we should never have had any Southerners. A consummation devoutly to be wished? I can't say. I think not.

This illustration, though slight, is significant. A dominant attitude in the South holds the world in such high regard that it objects to any change unless the change goes unrecognized until after it has occurred and taken its place in the pattern. This doesn't make sense to your typical modern, enthralled as he is by change. And it makes less and less sense to Southerners. But it's still here. The South changes, like any society, in recent years even rapidly, but typically it doesn't like to admit it's changing, and it objects hotly to being told it must change. This explains much of the opposition to the Supreme Court's decision. There's a large pathos involved in this: a people eager for many reasons to deal with outsiders, but hoping in spite of everything to keep the innocence of Eden. (If anyone objects to the Eden reference, I remind him there was a snake there.)

Concern for the community is a major Southern concern. The emphasis upon manners, upon custom, upon an accepted way of doing things is an emphasis upon community. If you move continually among strangers, as in a great industrial city, there is little demand for any but the most rudimentary manners—and most of these have to be codified in law. You'll probably never see these passers-by again; they're merely the concrete embodiment of the abstraction *man*. But in a community, among neighbors, it's vastly different. These are the people you have to live with. As Robert Frost says, if you told the truth about them, you'd have none left. I remember a colored neighbor, indeed a tenant, and especially his dog. Months after I'd returned to the farm I'd saved up enough money to buy a piece of beef for stew. We left the meat overnight in the cooling-trough out at the artesian well. During the night my neighbor's trifling hound dog broke into the box and ate the meat I'd waited months for. I wanted to shoot him. But then I remembered I had to live with his owner, and so I desisted.

I know a Southern white woman—old school, and plantation background—whom I can see riding along the roads of her community, bowing deeply, graciously, smilingly to every Negro she meets. She is following explicitly the Southern code at its best. Granted that this formality belongs to the interracial etiquette, developed in part to ease tensions between the supposedly superior whites and the supposedly inferior Negroes. Yet the manners are touched with informality and suffused with friendliness. Abstract justice is not being done, and the prophet is right in crying "How long, O Lord!" But what is being done has goodness in it, and is bad only in implying a justice—and a peace—which does not really exist.

To what degree these customary modes of action are merely customary, to what degree they hide and express racial prejudice, is a nice question. To some degree they are merely customary. Mrs. M. L. Avary, in her book *Dixie after the War*, tells the story of a Southern woman arguing with some Northern white teachers about their habit of treating the Negro servants as equals. "Were I to visit relatives in Boston," she said, "the nice people there would, I doubt not, show me pleasant attentions. Were I to put myself on equal terms with their domestics, I could hardly expect it. The question is not altogether one of race prejudice, but of the fitness of things." This woman saw the situation largely in terms of class relations, mistress and servants. The basic error she made—which is the basic error the South made— was that she saw all the Negroes only as "our domestics," now and forever. This is an instance of the extreme conservatism of the South; custom is king. (Maybe it was, but it's going now, with cotton.)

This tendency to do the accepted thing is naturally most common among the well-to-do. Doing the accepted thing, they have arrived at prominence. Having now a larger economic and social stake in society than the less privileged, they may be less willing to change. It thus happens that these very people who from their training and position may be less prejudiced racially may be at the same time less willing to accept desegregation, not because it is desegregation but because it is change.

But even with this inertia, the South is changing; and, as all its changes are from a stratified, static society toward a fluid, dynamic society, the speed of change is continually accelerating. As a consequence, there is an increasing number of white Southerners who, maintaining segregation entirely, or almost entirely, from custom, are growing increasingly tired of maintaining it.

In the first place, they grow tired of carrying two sets of manners, one for whites, the other for Negroes. The world we live in isn't the simple world of our forefathers; we have to grapple daily, sometimes desperately, with protean forces. Why, then, we ask, make our lives unnecessarily complex by maintaining two sets of customs? When we are doing this mainly from habit, we feel a strong tendency to stop it, in order that we may have more energy for the massive problems of life.

In the second place, these same Southerners may also be growing tired of the segregation pattern itself, and of the superior-inferior philosophy of life which it expresses. They are becoming more democratic; and as they become so in spirit, they desire that their customs and institutions should conform to that spirit. As segregation does not conform, they would prefer to let it go and treat all their fellow citizens alike.

The final objection to supporting segregation simply because it's customary grows out of one aspect of our world. If the world were moving in the slow pace of custom, the keeping of segregation for custom's sake would be more justifiable. But it's doing just the opposite; its mood is revolutionary, and more than ever we are a part of it. To strain and dislocate our lives with the maintenance of a great standing army, and with the building here in the heart of the South of such a world-shaking business as the Savannah River Project while at the same time holding on to a troublesome and increasingly trouble-making habit simply because it is done, suggests a degree of social schizophrenia which I am sure has not yet overcome us.

The young people especially are growing tired of keeping segregation for purely customary reasons. Their lives uprooted by military training, their experiences increasingly those of a desegregated society, they are decreasingly concerned about it. For them the problem is being solved, as most problems are, by being forgotten, or rudely dismissed, as was the case with the little boy in a strongly segregationist community who exclaimed to his parents: "When are you all going to stop talking about segregation!"

But segregation may have also, in addition to its customary value, a symbolic value.

In the most general sense, a symbol is something that stands for something else. All words are thus symbols. So is the word *segregation*. But it isn't the word we're defending, it's the thing. Some symbols, either words or things, have high emotional value; they are "charged." *Segregation* is such a word, the institution such a thing. They are both swathed in layers of emotion, and we defend the institution partly because it appears to us in this richly colored light.

Of what is segregation the symbol? What are the emotions that have attached themselves to it and make it valuable in itself? We can distinguish two groups.

The first is composed of those emotions whose source lies chiefly in the Reconstruction period and the years immediately following. Here we have the sense of white solidarity, the fear of black domination, the anger at the swift rise to power of an "inferior" race, the exhilaration of victory in the seventies, the satisfaction of the restoration of a copy of the old interracial order. It may seem strange that the passage of three quarters of a century has not dissipated these emotions. Perhaps the chief reason is that the white South has been laboring, though often unconsciously, to maintain segregation throughout this period; the emotions attendant upon its inception, therefore, have clung to it throughout the years.

The second group of emotions is closely connected with the first. By a perfectly natural process, the large complex of emotions connected with the Old South has attached itself to segregation, the continuing pattern of race relations.

What did the South save out of the Civil War and Reconstruction? What landmark stood above the waters? The relative position of whites and Negroes. Slavery was gone, but white supremacy and white control remained. Was anything else saved? Certain general values, perhaps, but no relationship so intact as this. Even agrarianism had received at the hand of industrialism a mortal wound, and Southerners, doubting the wisdom of their fathers in resisting industrialization, were adopting as they could the machines of the victorious North. Only the Negro remained in his place. Only the Negro, by remaining there, proved that the fathers had been right when they said he was inferior.

In that critical period, more than at any other time in its history, the South depended upon the Negro. Though the four corners of the Southern world had been shocked, he stood in his place—more than this, happily in his place, as our best writers assured us. Those were the days when Irwin Russell, Joel Chandler Harris, and Thomas Nelson Page filled our sore and longing hearts with pictures of the happy Negro: faithful servant and loyal friend, best product of the Old South. The picture was overdrawn. But we were desperate.

Is it at all strange, then, that segregation should have gathered about it from the beginning, and have maintained to the present, the pathos of a lost civilization? When we defend it, we defend the lives, hopes, customs of our fathers. This is the only thing we have left, the last beleaguered fortress of the Lost Cause. If we surrender it, who will remember what the Old South was? Indeed, who will be sure that it ever was? We defend it, therefore, as patriots who love their native land, as pious men who will not deny their past.

Listen to the tones of some of the older men. I have heard them. I remember an old farmer with some education, a good neighbor, a good citizen, a fox-hunter, a humorous man. He was talking about segregation. "You can take my property. I lost most of it in the Depression and I got most of it back. If I lost it again, I'd make a stab at it, even at my age. But take away the customs of my fathers, and I have nothing left to live for."

For some of us, therefore, segregation is a way of life, with all the sacred connotations the phrase implies. Is this sufficient reason for its defense?

The problem is one men face perennially, but not usually in so drastic a form. We are the products of the entire past. Moved by piety, we wish to preserve that past. Yet, for all his piety, every man has ideals that, though rooted in the past, point toward the future. Some of them he cherishes, others he discards. It is the South's misfortune that she lost so much so suddenly and has therefore been inclined to cling tenaciously to what she saved—in this case, segregation. The problem for us now is simply this: to what degree does segregation as a symbol, partly of Reconstruction, partly of the Old South, aid us in interpreting and living in our world? Any obligation we have to the past must be expressed in the present and directed toward the future. We cannot change the past, we can change the future. What help can the symbol of segregation give us as we face the future?

Like other symbols, its function is to clarify and focus life for effective action. If it is performing its function, it should help us to understand the world in which we live, outline within it the primary objects of our desire, and pursue those objects intelligently and successfully. Does segregation do this?

I think it is safe to say that it does just the opposite. Consider just one question: where in the world today, except in South Africa, does segregation help us to understand the world and to come to terms with it? Trying to hold in our minds this pattern as we look out upon the world, we are filled with utter confusion. Nobody seems to know what we're talking about. Everybody's talking Dutch—except, ironically, a handful of Dutch in South Africa! The language of segregation, of white supremacy, is almost a lost language. Every day it becomes more outmoded. Every day we use it we become less able to understand the world and be understood by it.

Somewhat the same thing may be said about affairs here at home. Segregation makes little sense in the industrial and mechanical world into which we are speeding. If we wish to succeed here, we shall have to stop talking the language of an earlier world. Again, segregation becomes less and less the American language. We may hate to believe it, but the decision of the Supreme Court in regard to segregation is, by and large, the decision of the American people. The Southern Negro is perfectly aware of this; he knows that he has the heart of the country with him when he insists that we begin to talk to him directly, and not through the curtain of segregation.

Finally, the symbol of segregation does not focus correctly our own memories, and therefore makes us less efficient in organizing our resources. It is true we had slavery in the old South, and have had segregation in the new; but to hold on to segregation as the essential truth of our past is to make a sad mistake. Slavery and segregation have been means to certain ends, some of them good, some of them bad; but to feel that in the latter we have summed up the essence of Southern life is to do a grave injustice to our forebears and a great disservice to ourselves.

Our unfortunate tendency to see segregation as the symbol of a great and lost past is the chief example of the kind of error we make as we stand, today, between the past and the future: we are driving blindly into the future with minds blurred by images of the past. We have the will to advance, but the lamp of experience, which should guide our feet, needs trimming badly. This is the need for reflection we spoke of earlier.

CHAPTER ·IX·

From Livelihood
to Life: I

IF OUR SYSTEM of race relations, which without argument is deeply interwoven with our life, is as generally indefensible as it appears, how do we explain those admitted values of our life discussed in Chapter 3? Did the system have nothing to do with their creation? Or did they grow up in spite of it? Or, finally, are they its fruits?

Most of these values were established under slavery and can be understood only in that setting. This makes the problem easier for us, as race relations under slavery were far simpler than they became later under segregation. Because these earlier relations were primarily economic, or productive, we may expect them to be an important factor in the creation of Southern values.

To believe this, one need not become a Marxist and argue that ideal values are nothing but a window-dressing for economic facts. For what is production? It is man's necessary relation to the physical world, in which men co-operate in the primary task of wresting a living from nature. All other forms of human relationship are secondary. Unless one is going to believe that the making of a living, man's necessary relation to the earth, is a brute affair and that spiritual values are the creation of secondary relationships—which I am not—then one has to consider the mode of production of primary importance, not only as livelihood but also as life. What part did slavery play in the creation of the values we cherish?

Two of these, the pervasive love of the land and a general sense of neighborliness, can be dismissed without detailed consideration. Both of them are largely the product of an agrarian life, with its relatively wide and unoccupied spaces.

Somewhat the same thing may be said about Southern hospitality. Here, however, the connection with slavery is closer. Slavery lifted Southern hospitality to the status of a legend. For that legend is part of the legend of the Big House, and the courtly host, and the great avenue up which the welcome stranger rode. Slavery made possible the lavish hospitality of the South in a sufficient number of cases for the trait to be considered characteristic of the entire South. The chances are it was most characteristic of the great planters and the poor whites. The great planters entertained with sherry, bourbon, and the festive board, the poor whites with their timeless days and sowbelly and cornbread. The poor whites, of course, were as much the product of the slave system—and the land—as the planters were. To the latter the system brought rich lands and wealth; to the former, over the years, pine-barrens, hookworm-infested soil, and no shoes to protect them against that crawling plague. But, even as they had less work to do, they had less desire to do it, a greater desire for leisure, and an increasing willingness to share it with the stranger.

Hospitality can be run into the ground, as the South illustrated and, I suppose, occasionally illustrates still. It can become showy and ostentatious, an expansive manner fitted only to the wide piazzas and great columns of the Greek-inspired architecture that Thomas Jefferson brought to the new land. It bankrupted even Jefferson in the end. Yet it still remains a virtue; and, though the South has lost much of it, and though the myth was never matched by fact, it would be a poorer land that did not at least desire to leave the latchstring out and to welcome to its open piazzas a supposedly friendly world. I know the piazzas are going, partly because of that detail of industrialization, air-conditioning; but I know also there are many communities where the doors are never locked, and where men still feel that people are neighbors and therefore friendly.

Leisureliness, closely connected with hospitality, is also closely connected with slavery. Of course, someone may say, that's simple: the Negroes did the work, the whites had the leisure. This is indeed the basic fact, and it represents a situation that no one could reasonably defend.

We still defend it without reason, however, and indeed without admission, in our support of segregation. Down in Petal, Mississippi, Editor P. D. East, of _The Petal Paper_, remarked recently that "we have lived for years off the labor of the Negro, and now . . . we're just plain scared out of our wits. Some of us may have to go to work for a living. . . . Some of us right now

don't know where our next mint julep is coming from."
So passes the white man's leisure, with the frosted glasses
and the long afternoons on the cool piazzas.

But there is more to it than this. Though the slaves
didn't have as much leisure as the masters, they put an
equally high, if not a higher, value upon it. Witnessing
the enjoyment of leisure by the master class, they
naturally desired it for themselves. More important than
this was the nature of their work. It was, with some
exceptions, work at not too rapid a pace nor too long continued. They saw to it that it wasn't carried on at too
rapid a pace; the steady pressure of their wills against the
master's made him yield somewhat in his desire for production. Most masters found out fairly soon that too
rapid, hard, or long-continued work simply didn't pay.
It aroused too much rebellion. As a last resort, slaves
ran away, and, whether they came back or were caught
or not, the time absent was lost for good. There were,
of course, foolish planters who in passion or blind interest
drove their slaves to death, but they were exceptions.
I know there are reports, supported even by the historian James Ford Rhodes, that the sugar-cane planters
of Louisiana and Mississippi felt that it was cheaper to
work a slave to death in seven years and buy another
than to conserve the first slave's life. The more recent
historian Clement Eaton says that the evidence does not
justify such reports. There were, it is true, certain heavy
tasks that had to be done as rapidly as possible, as, for
instance, the processing of the cane on sugar plantations.
But the planters took care of this by giving the workers
extra allowances, especially of whisky; and the workers

tended to look forward to these periods as times of comradeship and festivity, though indeed of backbreaking labor.

Generally, the slaves rested as they worked. The sense of leisure never entirely forsook them. I don't say creative leisure; simply not work. Why should they work hard? No future beckoned to them as it does to the free laborer. The products they produced were not theirs, and, regardless of what they did, rations and clothing would continue, children be cared for, and old age protected. They worked, then, only as much as was necessary to keep the white man satisfied.

All this developed in them a sense of irresponsibility, of relative unconcern for the material world, even, perhaps, of playfulness. The lightheartedness and good humor of the slaves has often been commented upon. This may have been partly a result of their native pliancy and resiliency, partly a shield against the realization of their own tragic condition, but it was doubtless also a result of the conditions of their work: so far as material goods went, there was little to worry out.

To suppose that this attitude did not react upon the whites is to suppose a high improbability. We accommodate ourselves to the people with whom we associate. In a sense, the white man taught the Negro how to work and the Negro taught the white man that work wasn't too important.

As for the Southern sense of place, or status, this is part of the entire feudalistic order, with its emphasis upon grades of society. Slavery was probably the chief cause of this order: it divided society into two grades, slaves and free men; and, in making society highly conservative, it made it a status society.

The last characteristic of the South which we need to relate to its base in slavery is our stress upon courtesy or, more generally, manners. The general structure of the South led it to emphasize living itself, and the manner of living—that is, manners. Take the Big House, itself the creation of slavery. People who build and approve such houses indicate a large interest in living. For them it isn't simply a place where you sleep, but the central scene of your life, a sort of stage upon which you play a part. The formality of the upper class in the South was closely related to this stage. One who has seen the gray moss hanging like a frieze about old Southern houses will not wonder that the dwellers there found a certain manner appropriate to their surroundings; nor, riding at night down a long avenue and seeing, suddenly, white columns shining out in the darkness, will he wonder that they moved sometimes like actors on a stage, repeating the proper words. They were still repeating the proper words in the 1860's until a Northern businessman taught them—most improperly but truly, and, alas, too late— that war was hell. A part of the present tragedy of the South lies in the fact that, upon a new stage, she is repeating the old lines.

But slavery also had a direct effect upon manners: they were in part developed for better control of the slaves. If it be objected that this merely adds insult to injury, consider a minute. It was indeed the glove hiding the mailed hand. But the South did not enslave Negroes to satisfy sadistic tendencies. No Genghis Khan rode here, nor too many Simon Legrees. The South enslaved

Negroes to produce more tobacco, rice, indigo, cotton, and sugar. Power undoubtedly brought out the brute in some Southerners, but, by and large, the planter kept his mind on the job of growing, let us say, cotton. He generally found that kindness grew more cotton than cruelty, and he often boasted that there hadn't been a whipping on his plantation in a long time. In the older and more settled areas, harsh treatment of slaves would bring upon the owner the severe condemnation of his neighbors. Again, it should be remembered that the Southern planter thought of himself as a Christian. He might justify slavery as the patriarchal organization illustrated in the Old Testament; in this view, he was the "father" of all these people, responsible to God for them. It would never have occurred to him to justify cruelty, except as a disciplinary measure.

Therefore, he had many incentives to extend the gloved hand, few to extend the mailed fist. But suppose it be admitted that both masters and overseers, from prudence or a touch of Christianity or both, tried to treat the slaves with some regard for their feelings—that is, as persons—and, certainly in the more intimate relations of the home, to stress courtesy in their relations with them. It may still be charged that such courtesy clearly suggested the superior-inferior relationship and was therefore bad.

This raises the question of what is good manners. Now, I must admit that, looking out upon the world with, I hope, fairly level eyes, I don't like an etiquette a part of whose purpose is to place me above or beneath another. But, then, I speak from the point of view of 1957, not 1857. Manners have to do with the customary

relations of human beings. The first requirement is that
the people in question agree generally as to what the
relationship is. Such an agreement existed under slavery:
the whites were evidently superior, the Negroes inferior,
and both groups accepted the situation. In this situation,
how could you avoid the etiquette of inequality? To use
the manner of equality along with the fact of inequality
would surely be false and ineffective. We ought not to
have had slavery; but, given slavery, one either develops
the manners suited to it or becomes a barbarian.

But one may admit this and still contend that the
existence of the master-slave etiquette made the manners
of free men impossible. Historically, this doesn't seem to
have happened. I know that ante-bellum whites are reported to have been self-willed, overbearing, and insolent, and are said to have got that way from associating
with slaves. I don't doubt that these were Southern
faults—and perhaps still are—and I imagine they were
related to the fact of slavery. But I doubt if Southerners
were typically insolent scoundrels. Nor are we safe in
assuming that the master-slave etiquette would necessarily prevent the formation of an equal-with-equal
etiquette. The possession of good manners, or, let us say,
of skill in manners, is the possession of skill in human
relationships. In a sense, the person with good manners
treats all people alike, as all are alike in being human; but
he also treats all people differently, as they are all different. It might well be the boast of such a person that he
knew how to get along with anybody.

Whether he boasts about it or not, the feeling is
there. For good manners is a skill, and men are happy
in possessing and using skills. This brings us to the root

of the matter and, curiously, to an underground passage leading to the problem of industrialism. The South found in human beings cheap productive capital. In order to ensure their continued use, it enslaved them. But then it had to develop skill in handling them. Finding force relatively unprofitable, it developed persuasion. But it didn't have much to persuade them with. There were certain bonuses—a chew of tobacco, a drink of whisky, a cut of calico—and, of course, gifts and presents at Christmas; but, because they were slaves and had already been bought and paid for, not wages. Therefore the South developed words; it developed manners. From this point of view, the manners of the ladies and gentlemen were in part the fine flower of that rough courtesy which got the cotton picked and the cane ground.

The slaves were happy to learn the words. That the words were spoken down to them didn't bother most of them: they considered that they were down. And, certainly, kind words were better than blows. Doubtless they often saw through their masters, but what was done fitted the situation, and generally they had accepted the situation. More than this, it fitted their deepest natures, for they seem to be a resilient, flexible people. They not only yielded themselves with some grace to the situation created by the white man, but they also must have found a native satisfaction, perhaps even delight, in teaching him how to act in the situation he had created. The manners the South has, she has learned mainly not only from slavery but also from the slaves—because they were slaves and, more than that, because they were Negroes.

The actress Fanny Kemble, for a time during the

1830's the unhappy mistress, by marriage, of a Georgia plantation, and no friend to slavery, suggests something like this. She speaks of "the natural turn for good manners which is, I think, a distinctive peculiarity of Negroes. . . . If it can be for a moment attributed to the beneficent influence of slavery on their natures (and I think slave-owners are quite likely to imagine so), it is curious enough that there is hardly any alloy whatever of cringing servility, or even humility, in the good manners of the blacks, but a rather courtly and affable condescension. . . ."

The North, in contrast to the South, very soon found machines operated by free men a more productive capital. It therefore developed skill with machines; it developed the mechanic. You don't have to be courteous to machines; given the technical knowledge, you can make them do what you wish. But the machines have to be run by men? True, and in a free society you persuade men mainly by wages. Indeed, in our sharply competitive modern society, men respond almost solely to wages and related material benefits. Furthermore, until about forty years ago, industry in the North had a mass of European immigrants pressing against the factory doors. You didn't have to bother too much even about wages. But even if this pool of labor hadn't always been cresting the dam, the fact would have remained that when you can offer wages to a worker you don't have to use as much verbal persuasion as when you can't. In brief, you don't have to have as much manners.

The slave-labor South had to have manners; the machine-labor North could partly dispense with them. Not that the North did dispense with them, for people are associated in other than productive relations, and even in machine production there is considerable human relationship. I am merely saying that when production depends almost entirely upon people you have to develop more skill in getting along with people than when it depends largely upon machines. You have to develop more skill in manners. The Southerner had to get along with people all the time; the Northerner mainly in off hours after he'd quit fooling with machines.

Now, I suppose our chief necessity in the world, and also perhaps our chief happiness, is to get along with people. I may seem to have argued earlier that it is to get along with nature—that is, to make a living—but I implied even there that we are social beings and that, from both necessity and desire, we establish human relationships. The Southern mode of production, however paradoxical it may seem, did prepare for that necessity better than the Northern.

Far better, perhaps. For when the Northerner, in off hours, turned from machines to the task of getting along with people, he ran into a difficulty that so far not all his ingenuity has been able to overcome. Though he can build machines with any kind of machine gearshift you want, he hasn't come up yet with a human gearshift that, as he leaves his job, would automatically throw him out of machine gear into human gear, out of skill into manners. As a consequence, he finds it difficult to treat people as people. He feels he can manipulate them, tighten a bolt here and loosen one there and, by a few adjustments, not of himself but of the others, get them to act as he wishes. Unfortunately, he has succeeded so well that few people are any longer shocked by this attitude. What once we blamed as propaganda we now praise as public relations. But there's still a hint of the mechanic fresh from the machine, with pliers and screwdriver, connecting human wires to get desired results.

It may be objected that there's no difference between the manipulative attitude of our Northerner and the persuasive attitude of our Southerner; both are trying to get somebody else to do something for nothing. I am willing to admit that Southern persuasion, especially on the master-slave level, is in part, perhaps in large part, manipulative. The difference is that persuasion, exercised between concrete individuals who know each other, tends to become manners, valuable in part simply as the structure of human relations; while manipulation occurs between essential strangers, each an abstraction to the other, not between concrete individuals. Without wishing to defend Southern manners too much, I should say that, in Buber's phrase, they show somewhat more of the "I-thou" relation than does the manipulation referred to.

We have in the South, then, this queer situation: setting out frankly to exploit human beings, we seem to be exploiting them less than the free-labor North, which set out to exploit machines. If this is true, it will be because means are more important than we had thought, the dyer's hand is colored by the stuff he works in, and hell is paved with more than good intentions. But in the matter of intentions we shouldn't credit the North too much to the discredit of the South. The Northern colonists intended to use slaves just as heartily as did the Southern, but the venture didn't pan out; geography and climate were against it. Therefore, they sold the slaves to the South; and in the long and bitter winter season, as they could neither farm nor, at least with any great pleasure, hunt and fish, they sat indoors and learned to read and, more to the point here, to develop machines that would enable them to work faster through the short summer and also to use more advantageously whatever products earth or trade might bring them. Not having such expansive acres as the South, they looked out from Nantucket upon the watery fields and beheld there a vast and common meadow alive with fish, or an open road to the cities of other men; and they built their fishing-boats to harvest those fish and their trading-schooners, the slavers among them, to visit those distant cities. Fascinated by water, and hindered by Jefferson's embargo upon the sea, they turned their eyes upon their own noble rivers and brawling brooks, and saw the power going to waste there, and built mills to use that power. Then, especially with the rush of European immigration, the mill-owners—the planters of the North, if you please—got their chance at human exploitation, and I don't think anyone will deny that they took it.

As the dynamic industrial system of the North expanded, it began to press against the slave-labor system of the South. Partly because of this fact, partly also because of movements sweeping the Western world—democratic, equalitarian, humanitarian—the North began to criticize the South, which was itself expanding and was therefore a challenge, on the ground of the inhumanity of the slave system. We now agree it was inhuman: a lot of Southerners agreed then. You could see its inhumanity around the world. For the world, the Western world, was moving toward freedom, and slavery was by definition the lack of freedom; you didn't have to know anything about it to condemn it. But the South knew something about it; it also knew something, though always too defensively, about the condition of workers in the free North; and the South defended it. It was, of course, the South's bread and butter. But Southerners also said it was a way of life, and, curiously, it now appears they had something, though they were hardly in a position to say exactly what they had. Apparently, it was a productive system that, though frankly adopted for human exploitation, turned out to be not entirely exploitative but rather, though without intention, somewhat human. The masters found that they couldn't simply exploit the slaves; both business discretion and human nature forbade. The slaves had passions, wills, affections of their own, and owners had to consider these. Indeed, as slavery became more human, owners desired to consider these. No one wants unhappy workers around him, any more than a mechanic wants a squeaking machine. In fact, even less; for the squeaking machine reflects only upon the mechanic's skill; the unhappy worker reflects upon the employer's nature.

But this paradoxical goodness within slavery was insufficient to sustain the system. It failed because it could not produce as much goods as a free system, and because it was opposed by the temper of the West. In its very inception, it was ill-advised: the American colonists had, while still in Europe, largely outgrown slavery, but they let themselves be overtempted by the limitless raw material waiting to be converted into goods for the European market, and they took the quickest method available. But through two centuries, as they settled into the system and made it stronger, the winds of freedom rose in the Western world, until in 1865 the combined conscience and business acumen of that world, expressed now in the power of the North, put an end to the Southern system. In brief, the South bet on the wrong horse. What made her defeat more swift and certain— and the great South, out of which we have created the picture of the Old South, lasted only a third of a century —was that it was the very nature of this horse to be run in a world race: the South was producing, not for subsistence, but for world markets. If—let us imagine the impossible—she had remained to herself, completely isolated behind some modern Chinese Wall, she might have lasted a lot longer. But, having installed the system in order to trade with the world, the South was neither satisfied nor able to keep the system within bounds. She pressed as far north as climate and the North would let her, as far west as time permitted, and even played with the temptation of pushing southward into Mexico and Cuba. It was then that the North, backed by the Western world, stopped her. In 1865 a Southerner told Whitelaw Reid, the Northern journalist, that the South had been defeated by the Germans, the Irish, and Jesus Christ. He didn't think that Jesus was really on the other side; he merely meant that a lot of people on the other side did think so. As to the Irish and the Germans, they were mainly on the other side because there was little place for them in the slaveholding South, while the industrial North always had a place for them. There it is: morals and machines.

But, in addition to the values, certain evils were created incidentally by the Southern productive system, at least one of which is important at present. This is the Southerner's tendency to unanalytical thought, impulsive action, and violence.

Unanalytical thought and impulsive action are not essentially evil; they are, on the contrary, related to that mark of any good life, spontaneity. They have been evil in the South only because of their tendency to pass into violence.

Parenthetically, Southern violence is also frontier violence. The South has been and still is a frontier. But Southern violence is more than this. It is, indeed, the base upon which we built our society. For we built it upon slavery, and slavery, however humanized by the grace of God, was established by violence and maintained by the threat of it. This was the smoldering volcano upon the slopes of which we built the Great Houses.

Partly to contain the flames of that volcano, the South cultivated good manners, human relationships. As the years passed, the manners became more suave, and it became increasingly impertinent to ask what lay beneath the smooth surface. Not only impertinent; it was also unnecessary. The South was in its very structure conservative. Living in such a society, Southerners developed habits, manners, good manners. But the skill of good manners depends upon both customary actions and basic agreement. The Southerner inclines to be agreeable as long as basically he agrees with you; and, living in a society where differences of opinion are not only not valued but are indeed frowned upon, he's inclined to believe he does agree with you. He will therefore put himself out to make the relationship easy and pleasant;

he will make himself agreeable. But if you probe to a level where exist the "realities" upon which all Southerners agree, and indicate a disagreement there, he will quickly become disagreeable. He has never considered the idea that there might be such disagreement, and he has therefore no practice in lifting these realities into the light of reason. Therefore he becomes disagreeable, and is apt to become violent. You have tapped the core of the volcano, and smoke and fire issue forth.

So the South became violent toward those in its midst who in the late antebellum days condemned or even questioned the Southern order; and so, urged on by its Barnwell Rhetts and its William Yanceys, it became violent toward the North in '61. Given the Southern character as it had been developed under its own economic and social system (and of course the opposing system of the North), the war probably was inevitable. A people better trained to examine the basic assumptions of their lives, however, might have been able to avoid a conflict that a great number of them did not want.

Thus, when the South defended slavery as a part of its way of life, it wasn't entirely mistaken: the productive system itself, though relatively uneconomic and from our point of view morally wrong, did produce certain good fruits. Slavery, however, has been gone for a century. What has happened to these fruits? Has segregation continued to produce them? Or are we living upon inherited capital, with no plans to replace it?

CHAPTER · X ·

From Livelihood
to Life: II

APPARENTLY, SINCE 1865 we have squandered vast amounts of that capital. Given our history before 1865 and the world since, this wastefulness, however regrettable, is natural. We have been living for ninety years now in a transitional, even a revolutionary, period, and our uncertainties and confusions have cost us dearly, especially in the values we have been considering. For such values are products of a basic orderliness.

This description of our times may sound unconvincing. For we tend to accept, with all its balances and stresses, the society into which we are born. As pre-Civil War days lie beyond our experience, we cannot compare them with ours. Indeed, even the days before World War I lie beyond the experience of many of us, and we have no immediate sense that times were different then.

I can remember clearly those halcyon days. And though, as I understand them now, they were both uncertain and dangerous, as I remember them they were stable. And I imagine that my father, who had been born in 1864, also thought of them as stable. Following as they did the stormy period of segregation and disfranchisement, they may very well have suggested to him that the race question had been settled. There's a parable of my boyhood that is suggestive here. On the 8th of May 1902, my sixth birthday, I sat quietly at a little table in our back yard and, as a token of special privilege, drank my first cup of coffee. At the same moment, in Martinique, Mont Pelée was in eruption and forty thousand people were being smothered and roasted to death. I knew nothing about it, however, either then or for a long time afterward. Nor about the race problem. Utterly at peace, I sipped my coffee on the slopes of the volcano.

The power surging beneath was in part the result of the conflict between the old Southern way of life, the agrarian, and the new way, the industrial. Manufacturing had raised its head feebly in the South from its beginning in America; in antebellum days it had been strong enough to make a few men question the Southern dependence upon the master crop, cotton, but not strong enough to challenge that crop. Small-scale factories had appeared as early in the South as in the North and for a time had multiplied as rapidly. Governor Williams of South Carolina in the first quarter of the nineteenth century not only practiced and urged crop diversification but also built on his plantation a five-story factory for the manufacture of cloth and hats. But the tide was against him. With the westward sweep of the cotton plantation about 1820, and with the turning of the Northeast from commerce to manufacturing, the South fell behind. William Gregg built in 1846 the first true cotton mill in the South; but, according to Broadus Mitchell, an authority in this field, Gregg was unable even by both precept and example really to establish before the war the cotton-mill tradition in the South.

The South was defeated partly because of her economy, as William Gregg had warned her, if it came to war, she would be. She had trusted that King Cotton would have the support of loyal subjects abroad; she had been mistaken. England wanted cotton, but wouldn't go to war to get it. The South, beleaguered, took up the production of arms, and made tremendous progress. In 1865, according to Whitelaw Reid, she was casting heavy guns at Selma, Alabama, as fine as the North could cast in her best foundries. But she had begun too late. Northern machines ran over Southern manhood. This fact, whenever it should be recognized, would suggest to the South the need for industrialization. It should not be surprising that the need was not recognized immediately, for the ears of the South were still ringing with the shock of war; and, besides, what could be done without capital?

As the need became clearer, however, and as the possibility increased, the South turned, and has continued with growing assurance to turn, toward industry. She hardly knew, however, what she was getting. She hardly knew that the coming of industry would mean, unless checked, the coming of industrialism, with all the ills she herself had indicated in the pre-Civil War arguments. She wanted the smokestacks upon a thousand hills; she didn't see that the paths among them would constitute a new way of life.

Or perhaps she did, but vaguely. Henry Grady's advocacy of the New South, meaning an industrial South, met some opposition. The present director of the South Carolina Planning and Development Board says it was still meeting opposition in some South Carolina towns as late as 1945: they just didn't want to be bothered with industries. (Today, he says, they're clamoring; Henry Grady has at last arrived, even in South Carolina.) This opposition of inertia also existed in Grady's time, together with the more reasonable opposition that the coming of factories would somehow change our life. It was doubtless this realization, vaguely apprehended, which dramatized the idea of the Old South at the very time Grady was popularizing the idea of the New. This tradition took form in the writers of the period, most influentially in the stories of Thomas Nelson Page. The war had been over twenty years; its bitterness had been mellowed by time, its action hallowed by defeat; and now the actors began to shine like gods in the glare of battle. Reconstruction was also over, the Negro back in his place and ready for apotheosis.

But even more significant than the creation of the Old South is the fact that among its creators were the men who were building the New. Apparently they compensated for the smokestacks they imagined upon the hills of the future by the mansions they imagined upon the hills of the past. For they imagined them, not only along the coast and the lower stretches of the great rivers, but scattered across the entire South in a profusion that had never been matched in fact. With these pictures of the Big House rose other pictures out of the golden age: the happy Negroes in the cottonfields, the banjos and voices from the quarters on moonlight nights—and the moon was always full—the hoopskirted young ladies swaying down the hall on the arms of gallant men, the tall glasses, the frosted bowl, the smiling Negro butler, and in the yard the Kentucky thoroughbreds saddled or grazing in the near-by pasture. We planted cotton all the way from Charleston to Lexington, Kentucky, then, and rode Kentucky thoroughbreds on every plantation clean back to Charleston—and the plantations stretched all the way!

However incongruous, the myth and the dream arose together. Henry Grady delivered his notable address on the New South before the New England Society, in New York, on December 22, 1886. Just six months before, on Sunday, May 20, the Louisville and Nashville Railroad, using the labor of eight thousand men, had shifted one of its rails along a two-thousand-mile stretch to make the width conform to the Northern gauge, thus symbolizing the union of Northern and Southern industry. In 1889 the United Confederate Veterans, which had existed in local groups from the end of the war, was organized on a South-wide scale. In 1895, the year of Atlanta's great industrial exposition, the women of the South met in that city, the industrial capital of the New South, and organized the United Daughters of the Confederacy. There, in the New York of the South, where if anywhere Southerners chaffered and traded like Yankees, Southern womanhood dedicated itself to keeping alive the South's great story. Thus turning half-consciously but with increasing eagerness toward a new way of life, the South still looked with averted glance upon idealized aspects of the old, most of which had never really happened, at least not in that remembered light, and none of which could come to life again under skies darkening with the smoke of mills and foundries.

Not only has the South been slow to make up its mind as to what sort of productive order it wanted, it has also been uncertain about the Negro's place in that order. Even while shifting from an agrarian to an industrial order, it has generally thought of the Negro as continuing in the agrarian. Apparently the South has thought it could achieve a balanced economy by letting the whites do the manufacturing and the Negroes do the farming. Such an idea would have been natural enough as an extension of the antebellum belief in a graded, static society, but would prove unworkable in the postwar dynamic society.

It isn't surprising that the white South thought of the Negro merely as farm labor. He had participated only slightly in the limited antebellum industry, and some of this participation had apparently been a failure, though the cause was probably poor management rather than the worker's inability. The South, however, got the fixed idea that the Negro was not suited for industrial work, and, therefore, in its struggle toward industrialization, it has largely overlooked him.

In fact, in the first wave of industrialization, the building of the cotton mills in the eighties and nineties, it very pointedly overlooked him. The motives behind the building of these mills—financed largely by Southern capital—were both selfish and patriotic. The leaders of the white South, seeing many white farmers driven down to the economic level of the Negroes, and fearing that they might be driven into the arms of the Negroes, built the mills partly because of patriotism—white patriotism, that is. They did not, however, overlook the profit. With wages around twenty-five cents a day, net profits often ran from forty to sixty per cent. Regardless of mixed motives here, racially their intentions were evident: they built the factory for the whites and kept the Negroes in the furrow. Today some of these factories are building tractors, and the poor plowhand, elevated to the tractor seat, is gaily sideswiping the crop or running the tractor up trees. As soon as he learns better, he goes to town to drive a truck or up North to get him a factory job.

In brief, an industrial order knows nothing about the Negro's place, or, indeed, any man's place, and less than nothing about an ignorant farm laborer using simple tools. Furthermore, an industrial order becomes increasingly complex, and therefore demands, at least in certain areas, increasingly skilled and responsible operatives. Among such men arise economic and political leaders, who carry with them the tenders of the simpler machines. That the South of the 1880's was unaware of this is not surprising; but its ignorance has retarded its economic development and encouraged the growth of racial attitudes that might otherwise have been avoided.

Uncertain as to whether we favor agrarianism or industrialism, uncertain also about the Negro's place in industry, we are most uncertain in our confusion of race relations with labor relations.

Under slavery, the relations of whites and Negroes were mainly productive, economic, or labor relations. After the war the white South took up first the problem of labor relations, but was distracted from it by the events of Reconstruction and became involved in the morass of race relations. Out of this period came segregation. It seems impossible to tell to what degree segregation exists for economic reasons, to what degree for racial. We have seen that the two motives are all tangled together.

In so far as segregation exists for productive rather than racial purposes, and in so far as it is generally accepted by those involved, it may be expected, like all productive orders, to produce human values. Significantly, segregation is less glaring in the productive field than anywhere else. The reason is immediately apparent: to separate whites and Negroes entirely in this field is to make it extremely difficult for the whites to exploit the Negroes or even to have any control over them. Therefore, Negroes move in and out of white society on the economic level, often working beside whites, in their homes intimately, upon only one condition: the work of the Negro must be subordinate—or at least his attitude must be subordinate. This injection of race relations into the basic productive pattern opens the way for economic discrimination.

The fact that segregation is least evident in the productive area suggests that its purpose isn't primarily productive but racial. Where production isn't involved, it is applied more strictly. As the productive system is the chief generator of human values, we can hardly expect much incidental goodness from the system of segregation. Especially is this true when we consider the further fact that it was never deeply accepted and certainly isn't now. If the Negro accepted himself as inferior, deserving therefore a separate and inferior place, he would remain satisfied so long as no disruptive elements were injected. For he would hardly recognize the exploitative and wasteful aspects of the system.

But such naïveté is simply impossible today. The Negro becomes increasingly less inferior and increasingly more aware of the fact. He therefore becomes increasingly dissatisfied with his place in the segregated productive system; and the system becomes increasingly unstable under the pressure of his dissatisfaction.

When we add to this cause of instability the fact that the South is changing its productive system from ignorant hand labor to skilled machine labor, we see immediately that the limited segregation of the Negro in the productive field is doomed by the very demands of the system we are adopting.

But when we consider segregation in its main, non-productive, non-economic aspect as a special instrument in the field of race relations, we arrive at even more extreme conclusions. In this field, segregation is maintained simply to separate whites and Negroes on the basis of supposed superiority and inferiority, and to keep the Negroes aware of inferiority. (We gloss this over with talk about "differences," but we feel superior.) This is to make separation itself a principle of social order—an end, not a means. Down this road chaos lies. Yet this is the road the South has chiefly followed under segregation.

To segregate a group of people according to their jobs may have some justification. In a sense, all men are separated by their jobs; and if there is a group especially fitted for a certain kind of work, that work will set that group somewhat apart from the rest. Nevertheless, all men are bound together by their work, because work is a social activity. Through work each of us has a part, whether just or not, in the social order. But to segregate people simply for the purpose of pushing them back and down and seeing them there is a barbaric impulse that, if indulged in, will destroy the social order. It is probably impossible for people so discriminated against not to realize it for what it is: a direct attack by persons upon persons which can only result in a widening social chasm and in the undermining of personality on both sides. For persons come into being in society; and where a social chasm exists, personalities are thwarted on both sides, though in different ways, regardless of which group is responsible for the chasm.

Yet even while doing this socially destructive thing the white South was educating the Negroes, and permitting them to be educated by Northern philanthropy, in democratic ideals and in the habits of industry, and was thereby permitting bridges, however frail, to be thrown across the chasm that racial animosity had opened. The common sense and the democratic and Christian ideals of the South were, though slowly, bringing together again the two races that segregation had so rudely thrust apart.

With such currents of change as we have described running violently in the South for almost a century, undercutting old institutions and clashing with one another, it would be surprising indeed if we had maintained untarnished the values created in the Old South. Doubtless we have added some, for freedom itself is a value, and Negroes—and whites too—are no longer bound in chattel slavery. But we seem to be in the process of losing others.

Chief among the old values was a regard for manners—at its best, courtesy—and a sense of place. Both of these are natural in a conservative society, but find precarious rootage in a progressive society. It is especially precarious when social change is as revolutionary and in its several currents as conflicting as it has been in the South for a century.

Perhaps courtesy was the most delicate flower of the Old South, and perhaps it has suffered most. Perhaps it was inevitable that it should suffer most, being the most delicate, the most Southern, in the wintry un-Southern weather of many years now. That it has suffered is suggested by the disgraceful actions of white students toward a single Negro student, a girl, in Charlotte, North Carolina, recently. Regardless of whether anyone thought the girl should have been there or not, she was evidently a quiet, reserved person, and the actions of some of the white students toward her were barbaric.

Talk about segregation being the Southern way of life! It was the long influence of segregation upon those white children which made them betray the essential South: the South of the kindly heart and the reserved manner.

The deterioration of Southern manners since the Civil War is due most of all, though by no means entirely, to the fact that there has been no basic agreement between whites and Negroes. The whites have generally supposed that such an agreement existed. We have described segregation in pleasant terms, and as for much of the time most of the Negroes have tacitly accepted the situation, we have assumed we were telling the truth. They, however, were silent only because complaint was unhealthy. They could never believe in their hearts what under slavery they do seem to have believed—that the superior-inferior relations of segregation were true and right. Emancipation and Reconstruction had given them the idea of equality. Under an imposed segregation the whites tried to remove that idea from their minds, but in the context of the Fourteenth Amendment, a democratic nation, the educational and economic advantages of the Negroes, and, indeed, the conscience of the whites, the attempt failed.

If it had succeeded, if the Negroes had forgotten their taste of equality, if the nation had entirely forgotten them, and if the white South itself had forgotten its faint twinges of conscience, an excellent code of manners might have developed. None of these things happened, however. Manners grew worse, and for a long time the South was swept by violence.

This violence showed itself in all the forceful methods used to bring people into line either with the dominant group or with some headstrong individual. The general feeling was that everybody had to agree even though you had to kill him to make him agreeable. The methods ranged all the way from threats, through beatings and murders, to mob actions and lynchings. Though most of the violence was directed by whites against Negroes, who needed most of all to be made agreeable, it didn't stop there but was continually spilling over among the whites and Negroes separately. Much of it, of course, was simple frontier violence. Much,

however, was the natural accompaniment of the breakdown of manners among a people who had lived by
manners. During my boyhood, my father often carried a
pistol when he left the farm; and the auditor's annual
report for the state of Georgia about the turn of the
century shows the returned value of all agricultural
implements as slightly less than the returned value of all
weapons.

But the deterioration of Southern manners isn't
due solely to the lack of basic agreement between the
races. Another important cause is the transfer of leadership, during the last quarter of the nineteenth century,
from the aristocrat to the common man. Since that time
the South has often been controlled by men who have
lacked a tradition of public manners. In private, in the
give-and-take of daily life, they may be essentially as
well-mannered as the old aristocrats. In public, however, in dealing with the problems of society, they show
a lack of imagination and sometimes a brutal determination to attain their ends by any means whatever. They
simply overlook manners; they have a poor sense of the
occasion, and of the fitness of things. They speak rudely,
as the South Carolina legislature did in 1944 in its (futile)
attempt to keep the Negroes out of the primaries, and
as more than one legislature has done since 1954. Defending, so they say, the Southern way of life, they
indicate by their actions that they have lost its quality.

That earlier legislature was the one which shocked
me into a public statement, not on justice but on manners. Perhaps, as a Southerner, I felt that we'd had
injustice with us for a long time and might have it a
while still, but that bad manners were of today, our

continuing creation. Furthermore, the damage they do is mortal. To steal a man's economic or political right is to damage him in his position and perhaps, indirectly, in his person. But to undermine his manhood by refusing to speak of him as a man is to strike at the core of his being. I think I was right in being shocked at such manners.

In spite of the vulgarization of manners, the crumbling of manners into violence has decreased with urbanization, better police protection, and improved race relations. Many white Southerners feel that these relations have grown worse since the Supreme Court's 1954 decision. They have grown worse only in the sense that they have been diminished; some communication has been lost; but this diminishing is the necessary preliminary to the substitution of other and better relations. Better because truer to the facts. The old interracial manners are rapidly breaking down; the new are being slowly substituted.

We are in the process of substituting an etiquette of equality for one of inequality. The change is especially difficult because in the South changes have ordinarily been made slowly and even imperceptibly. In a folk society, such as the South to a degree was, folkways do take precedence over state ways; laws follows custom. But what we fail to recognize is this: the South is daily becoming less a folk society and more an industrial society. Daily, therefore, custom is becoming less important and law more important. Daily, abstract justice is of more concern, concrete habits of less. The demand that the South change, perhaps rather sharply, its customs is simply the demand that it act in the fashion of the industrial society to which it aspires and which it is rapidly becoming.

In the Supreme Court decision, therefore, the growing demand of justice is being urged against the weakening demand of custom. The demand for justice exists not simply in that decision, but also in the hearts of both Negroes and whites. It is this demand, among other things, which is breaking down the old interracial etiquette of inequality and substituting therefor a new etiquette of equality. We are revising our lives to satisfy common ideals and needs.

It is possible to sketch the revision. The white people of the South will tend to treat the Negro as an equal as he becomes an equal in law and in fact. Given just laws, his becoming an equal depends both upon his own achievements and attitudes, and upon the attitude of the whites. Southern whites, at least in theory, consider other whites their equals. We have learned this over centuries, following the democratic ideal and also expressing the now outmoded need for white unity against Negro slaves and freedmen. Ideally, we should grant the Negro the privilege accorded the white, and in the democratic spirit accept him as an equal because he is a man. We will not do this immediately, however, being still enslaved by the phantom need to protect ourselves against him. Accordingly, we make him prove his equality. This he is proceeding, and now rapidly, to do. As he gains economic power, he moves toward equality in economic relations. He is already equal in a detail of our financial life: at the bank counter he is plain John Doe. He is rapidly becoming an equal in the world of merchandising: all folding money is green. As he gains the ballot, he will become a political equal. As he gains legal support, he moves toward equality in civil relations. It is here that he is now moving most rapidly; and it is here that the concept of justice, growing ever stronger in our minds, supports the decisions of the courts.

And now, as the Negro gains equality, he will tend to accept himself as an equal, and this will put added pressure on the white man to accept him. For to some degree we accept every man's evaluation of himself. We may not particularly like to, but when men meet to do business they are fairly realistic. That Southern whites and Negroes have to do business together is a foregone conclusion, and, though the white may prefer to deal with "Uncle Tom," if it is necessary he will deal with "Mr. Jones." (For this is the commercial South of 1957, not the patrician South of 1857.) Recently, in a Southern town where a boycott between the races had been going on for some time, the mayor and his Citizens' Councils associates agreed to deal, not with the "Uncle Toms" of the community, but with the leaders of the NAACP. It is true that the conference, though amicable, got nowhere. The significant thing is that it was even held, for it was a recognition by the whites of the kind of force they were up against and a willingness to accept that force and confer man to man.

The refusal of men to be treated as inferiors is the essential step toward their being treated as equals. Basic equality is equality in manhood, not in economics or politics or social position.

This transitional period in manners may last for a good while. The whites who from their own assured positions are the best able to treat Negroes as equals will be the first to do so, and even they will be inclined to limit such treatment to those Negroes who have more than average ability. The whites who are the least able to treat Negroes as equals, those who depend most heavily upon actual and supposed Negro inferiority, will be the last to do so; and it's hardly worth guessing to which Negroes they will first extend the prize, if one may call it that, of equality.

It appears, then, that segregation has neither created new values nor even maintained the finest values of the Old South. Its passing, therefore, may clear the way for the coming of a more democratic society through which, if we are both wise and fortunate, we shall be able to create values comparable to the finest in our past. Meanwhile, we should be cheered by the fact that there is a rich life in the South which flows around and sometimes submerges the islands of racial isolation. In spite of the worst we have done, this is still a good place to live. It will grow better as we understand it.

CHAPTER XI

The Massive, Concrete South

As THE SOUTH LOSES certain characteristics of a folk society and adopts others of an industrial society, it finds itself dealing increasingly with abstractions, such as justice, and depending less, therefore, upon customs and manners. Many a Negro who used to go to his "white folks" for help now goes to law—and partly because he hasn't any white folks left to go to. The South is uneasy because of the growing importance of abstractions generally. Robert Penn Warren, in his recent book *Segregation*, refers to this uneasiness as "the instinctive fear, on the part of black or white, that the massiveness of experience, the concreteness of life, will be violated. . . ."

This fear has had wide expression in the last three years in adverse comments on the segregation decision of the Supreme Court. We are told that it was based upon psychological and sociological theories (abstractions), and not upon the hard facts of law; that, in addition, these theories were based upon one or more *isms:* socialism or even communism. The fear of *isms* is

nothing new in the South (my uncle feared even ideal-
ism); the Supreme Court merely touched it off. And the
truth of the matter seems to be that the fear is, in general,
a salutary one, especially for a conservative people such
as the Southerners, who are advancing rapidly into that
pathless forest of abstractions, the modern world. The
only trouble is, we can't back out of the forest, and
only by arriving at some better abstractions shall we be
able to cut our way through it. What do we in the
South know about abstractions?

We know we are afraid of them. We've been afraid
of them now for about a hundred and forty years. We
called them *isms*. In antebellum days they included—I
speak almost at random—humanitarianism, socialism,
communism (yes, even then, though not of the Marxian
variety), feminism, and, worst of all, abolitionism.
Feminism would have taken the dear ladies off the
pedestals, and we weren't quite ready for that; they
have since come down.

Now, all these *isms*—indeed, all *isms*—seemed to
come from the North, a natural breeding-ground. Even
Darwinism, that late-nineteenth-century danger, came
by way of the North. We knew of course, that Darwin
was an Englishman, and didn't blame the Yankees
directly for him. Indeed, we didn't credit the Yankees
with all the diabolisms they retailed. We knew that many
of them were spawned in Europe; but the main ports of
entry were Boston and New York, where European
isms were welcomed along with all those other un-
American characters, the immigrants. The Yankees kept
the immigrants for the factories, but, being traders, they
tried to retail to us—at a profit—the various *isms* they

imported. Toward the close of the century they were trying to sell us radicalism and, in religion, the higher criticism, and even atheism. They didn't have much luck with the religious goods, but, curiously, we bought one shipment of radicalism: the Northern radicals had dragged the Negro upstairs, the Southern radicals kicked him back outdoors and slammed the door in his face.

There's a striking recent instance of the South's accepting with outstretched hands a Northern *ism*, but there were reasons for this. I refer to the New Deal, which was headed by a gentleman from Hyde Park and "brain-trusted" by various gentlemen mainly from the Northeast. We took it, first, because we were hungry, bad hungry, and it brought food; second, because our own Democratic Party sponsored it; third, because Mr. Roosevelt, both from inclination and from a lack of theoretical interest, played down the theoretical, abstract side and let it remain for the most of us the concrete New Deal, not an abstraction, New Dealism. (Occasionally some wicked person so described it!) As we are no longer hungry, a good many of us have recognized the *ismatic* quality of the deal, and indeed have equated it with our old enemy socialism, now called "creeping."

Over the years, however, the South has been buying, mainly from the North, one *ism* so big, so attractive, so respectable, that for the most part we haven't recognized what we were buying. This is industrialism. To some degree, in both antebellum and postbellum days, Southerners did warn against industrialism as a threat to our way of life. But it has generally come with so little fanfare—except when we ourselves built the cotton mills —with so little statement of purpose—which was natural, the main purpose being to make money for the Northerners, and we Americans are a modest people when it comes to making money, especially out of somebody else—it came, as I say, so quietly, with here a smokestack and there a smokestack, saying nothing on the one important subject in the South, the race question—as it says nothing now—that as a rule Southerners never recognized it as an *ism*, and indeed don't so recognize it today.

Your Southerner is typically a realist. He will embrace practically anything life brings if it comes without benefit of theory; but if it comes waving a banner he is almost certain to grab his sword and, without further consideration, have at it. He's pretty short on theory, and what he's short on he's naturally suspicious of. How did he get that way?

Check back on the *isms* he has feared most of all, radicalism and abolitionism. Both were concerned with the Negro. The South feared these *isms* most of all because they tended to disintegrate its own essential *ism*, the one abstraction upon which its massive, concrete life had been built. What was this abstraction?

Slavery. Most Southerners, of course, never owned slaves. But, as the historian John Drayton of South Carolina said of his native state as early as 1802, slavery was the base upon which the South built both its power and its ideals. But slavery, you say, was a fact, not a theory; and it is interesting that even the form of the word suggests this. Perhaps we should call it an actual situation based upon and eventuating in a theory. A concrete abstraction. For who was this African whom planters were buying? Did anybody know him? Did anybody really care? Had the buyer seen him in his native home and complete manhood? We merely hoped he was the abstraction we wanted, manpower. With a climate moist and warm, with broad, rich lands and easily tilled staple crops, the early South lacked only manpower. From Africa, therefore, we abstracted the living individual, tearing him from his home and his culture, transporting him across three thousand miles of water, and landing him, if lucky, on these shores, so much manpower, to be bought and sold like horsepower. Having bought this manpower, we further stripped it of its language and, so far as possible, of its African memories, and then proceeded to build into it such simple traits as seemed most valuable to us. By a process of violent abstraction, we converted the African Negro into the image of our desire, a slave.

Upon this abstraction, upon the body of the slave, the South was built. The white South has never really forgotten this; on the contrary, with the passage of the centuries and the development of a humanitarian spirit both within and without its borders, it has felt a growing, though most of the time unadmitted, unease. It was afraid of abstractions, for one thing, because it had built its life upon an abstraction it couldn't justify. Oh, it tried, sometimes most philosophically. Often, however, it refused even to try, admitted that on the ground of justice the case was already lost, and defended only the excellence of the system as it existed, or the necessity for its continuation now that it had been established.

This was the attitude of the plantation doctor in his reply to a comment by Fanny Kemble, the actress. Said Mrs. Kemble: "I put all other considerations out of the question, and first propose to you the injustice of 'the system alone.' " "Oh," replied the doctor, "if you put it upon that ground you *stump* the question at once; I have nothing to say to that whatever, but"— and there followed "the usual train of pleadings—happiness, tenderness, care, indulgence, etc., etc., etc.—all the substitutes that may or may not be put up in the place of *justice,* and which these slaveholders attempt to persuade others, and perhaps themselves, effectually supply its want."

The South was also afraid because of its real ignorance of the man behind the abstraction. What was he thinking, this so docile Negro? Did he perhaps after all desire freedom? Might he be planning insurrection? Especially the free Negroes, beyond close observation —what might they be planning for themselves and the slaves? This fear became stronger after the insurrection in Charleston in 1822, led by the free Negro Denmark Vesey. The South has always insisted that it understood the Negro, but in its less argumentative moments it says nobody understands him. So in the Civil War diary of Mrs. Chesnut. On several occasions she tried pointedly to learn what her favorite servant, Lawrence, thought about the progress of the war and the prospect of freedom. It was useless. No one could read that expressionless mask. He was the perfect servant. But who was the solid man behind that abstraction?

In the long run, the South also feared abstractions, certainly theories about the nature of society, because it was too well pleased with the society it had created. Knowing the doubtful base upon which it had built, it feared that investigation might result in disaster—as one fears to probe the damage done by termites lest the house fall down. It was a strangely pleasant society. If one should suggest that this result was due to the grace of God, I should not disagree. (And I do this without agreeing that the South was doing the will of God by abstracting the Negroes violently from Africa.) Something about the land, something about the conditions of work, something about the temperament of the Negroes, something about the whites—well, that they were, nominally, Christians, for one thing—combined to produce a society that even today shows a sense of humanity and an appreciation of life not too common in the modern world.

When the planter bought the abstract, diagrammatic African, he bought essentially a machine, a stripped-down powerhouse. Into that machine he tried to build certain gadgets. The slave was to be docile, submissive, unreflecting. In general, he was to be inferior, and therefore by various methods he was made inferior. We naturally preferred that he be happy, both because he would be more effective thus, and because in spite of what we were doing we were still human. We therefore did certain things that tended toward his happiness, and we assured ourselves that he was happy. Happier, indeed, than free laborers, we told ourselves and others. The underground railroad, especially busy during the decade preceding the Civil War, made us a bit doubtful of our claims. The real shock came when, during the war, the Negroes joyfully accepted freedom in the occupied areas, and, after the war, throughout the South. Yet even this did not change our basic theory.

Thus the slave became a type, an idea bodied forth

in flesh and blood, an abstraction. Yet, because he was human, and perhaps because he was African, he neither was nor ever became the simple machine we thought we had bought. He was an individual, with temperament, desires, passions of his own; and the slaveowners, even the overseers, recognized this and, to some degree, accommodated themselves to it. Out of this strange and basically evil relationship arose certain values that we still cherish.

Commenting upon the ambiguity of slavery, which made property of a person, Frederick L. Olmsted remarked in the 1850's: "It is difficult to handle simply as property a creature possessing human passions . . . while the absolute necessity of dealing with property, as a thing, greatly embarrasses a man in any attempt to treat it as a person."

It is not surprising that the South, faced with this impossible task of distinguishing between the enslaved body and the free spirit, should have developed an other-worldly religion. A this-worldly religion would have ruined us. It might have led the whites to free the Negroes, it might have led the Negroes into fanatical insurrection or dying despair. Heaven saved us all.

But the old Southern fear of abstractions was not due entirely to the founding of the South upon a violent abstraction, nor to the paradoxical creation upon that abstraction of a rather satisfactory society. It was due also to the existence and progress of the North (with the added force of the modern world behind it). The land and climate of the North was less suitable to slave labor than that of the South. Northerners, then, with the same urge for success, set themselves to mechanical invention. From the rushing rivers they abstracted water power, and from the limited motions of the human body, eventually unlimited machine power. Thus, continually changing their way of making a living, they changed, and willingly, their society. Beginning—if one may repeat the old canard—by abstracting from the tropical nutmeg its color, shape, and pressure and thus creating the Connecticut nutmeg, they ended by abstracting the idea of society from all the busy interchange of daily life, and then proceeded to shape the daily life to the idea obtained. Then, being traders, again partly by necessity and later by the logic of the industrial system, the Yankees peddled their nutmegs and their sociological ideas wherever they could. As the South was close, colonial, and—except for its own God-given staple, cotton—unproductive, they peddled them largely in the South. The nutmegs made the South suspicious, but because it needed the goods it continued to buy. As for the *isms*, however, when the North really got to pushing these partial by-products of the industrial movement of the nineteenth century, the South simply refused: she had built her life upon one *ism*, the theory of slavery, and she feared properly that any other, however innocent, might end by uprooting that base.

Why did the North keep on abstracting while the South, after one violent effort, desisted? The reason probably lies mainly, first, in the total physical situation and, second, in the productive system adapted to it. In regard to the first, the North found it so hard to make a living that it overexerted itself and kept right on raising its standard without much thought of what it was doing. The South, on the contrary, found it so easy that it never took the job too seriously—perhaps never seriously enough. The South always had a slight tendency to stop where it was; and—a fact of more importance—its machines, the slaves, were always eager to abet it in this tendency. The Southern world, therefore, became and continued fairly concrete and massive. Southerners enjoyed it as it was; their machines, enjoying at least their inefficiency, refused to accept any abstraction beyond the original one. Besides, what else could be done? When the African had been reduced to manpower, there was little more you could do to him.

In contrast to this, and a second reason for the continued production of abstractions in the North, the physical machines of the North were subject to indefinite improvement; tinkering with them both sharpened the inventive mind and increased the profits. The first abstractions kept on proliferating, growing not only in number but also in complexity. The Southern machine, the slave, though he too proliferated, did not become more mechanical; indeed, he became less so and thus forced the master back toward human standards. The Northern machines became constantly more efficient, and, all unintentionally, the operatives, as Thoreau realized a hundred years ago, became more mechanical. Thus a gulf appeared and widened between the living man and his mechanical job, and society itself began to show the inner strain. There arose, then, as the result both of the abstract thinking in the machine world and of the need for social revision, social philosophers, sociologists. To these socially analytical minds the neighboring South, with its barbarous system of slavery, seemed in need of advice and revision. Maybe it was; but it was both too sound and too shaky to admit it; and so the Northern *ismatics* had to persuade the North to beat some sense into the South.

The venture, as is usual with such ventures, wasn't entirely successful. Slavery was destroyed, but the white South still saw in the freedman essentially the same image, or abstraction, it had seen in the slave. Having made the Negro thoughtless, improvident, and irresponsible under slavery, we found him so under freedom; and, because we still wanted him to be inferior in order that we might keep him in an inferior place, we were glad, even while complaining, that he was improvident and irresponsible—as the vulgarism puts it, "just like a nigger." Consequently, that phrase carries both complaint and amused satisfaction, a touch of god-like complacency, as who should say: *The Negro's in his place, and all's right with the world.*

But this second abstraction, "the Negro," is even more troublesome to us than the first one, "manpower." For the manpower abstraction did combine with management to create the essential South, and the co-operation thus involved clothed with considerable human meaning the bare abstraction. But the more recent abstraction "Negro" exists mainly not to bring men together in production but to separate them by race, and results therefore in mutual, though unequal, ignorance between the races. Just as the whites say "That's just like a Negro," so the Negroes say "White folks is white folks."

We thus see that, though enslaved manpower, the basic abstraction upon which the life of the South was

built, has been destroyed, we still lean heavily upon
another abstraction, racialism or racism. We aren't building our society about this *ism*, as we did in antebellum
days about slavery, but are on the contrary tearing our
society down.

    The Southern white, in dealing with a Negro, deals
partly with an abstraction, with his idea of the colored
race embodied in the man before him. This is suggested
by the frequency of his comment that he likes the Negro
in his place, although he never says that he likes the
white man in his place. Apparently there is something
attached to every Negro which is not attached to every
white man: the idea of a place. It may be objected that
there's no sense in a man's saying he likes the members
of his own race; that can be taken for granted. Unfortunately, it cannot. Whites do not say it in the South,
not because every white man likes every other, but
because historical conditions have made it unnecessary
for him to say so. One reason we insist we like the
Negro is that the outside world and our own consciences
have shouted and whispered that, in the light of our
treatment of him, we don't. But a more important reason
than this is suggested by the phrase "in his place." We
like him in his place. We like him for staying in his
place. The liking is a bonus for his staying there. We
don't have to give the white man any bonus for staying
in his place; the place itself is the bonus. The Negro's
place, being unattractive, has to carry a bonus with it.
Consequently, white people like or dislike other white
people for purely individual and personal reasons. With
one exception: if a white man, for some fool reason,
gets out of his place—fails, that is, to keep the Negro at

the proper distance, in the place he belongs in, where he can be liked—we bestow upon him our deepest dislike.

We like any Negro, then, just so long as he remains in the inferior position to which he has been assigned, as actual or potential servant. We do not like him as a man; indeed, we seldom see the solid, living man beneath the abstraction servant.

Since this abstraction, the Negro-as-servant, includes such an important part of Southern life, it is not difficult to see why the South, certainly the white South, fears abstractions. We fear the abstraction here partly because it leaves us in ignorance of the vaguely felt, solid man behind it, partly because our lives are built upon this abstraction and we are not sure it is correct: the Negro may not be the inferior being we assume he is, but an equal, as some *isms* have maintained and as our consciences increasingly suggest. This matter of naming correctly the powers surrounding us is of fundamental importance. The electrician knows it: is the line hot or cold? Men are always in danger, as the Bible warns us, of falling by chance into the hands of that supreme power, the living God.

These seem to be the reasons why the concrete, human, interlinked, and conservative society of the South, both because of its concrete values and because these values have been built upon an abstraction never entirely defensible and increasingly under attack from within our hearts and from without, is afraid of and opposed to abstractions. In the long run, the most powerful pressure against the abstraction "Negro" comes from within our hearts. Though the white South, in the creation of its massive, concrete life, tried to make the Negro an abstraction, the Negro, too wise ever to become merely that, got himself built into the manifold and daily life of the South until white Southerners, regardless of all their professions, sense vaguely in him the rich core of their lives.

But beyond this inner pressure in the whites to recognize the Negro for the solid man he is, certain outer developments are occurring which lessen our need for and fear of this basic abstraction, and so, perhaps, of abstractions in general. The greatness of the South did rest upon slave labor. But modern industrialism, with some aid from conscience, destroyed that social order, and now begins to show us how men may live generously and easily without oppressing the laboring class; to show us, indeed, that the entire society can advance only as all its members, its laborers included, advance also. Again, when the white South during Reconstruction struggled against that abstraction the Negro-as-dominant, and set up the opposing abstraction the white-as-dominant whatever the cost, it acted in the light of its history. Daily, however, that abstraction becomes less sensible and more confusing, both in the light of the Negro's advance in citizenship since 1876, and especially in the light of our increasing understanding of the demands and the rewards of industrialism. Increasingly, then, we shall let this outworn abstraction go, and, facing the coming industrial order with its multiplicity of new abstractions, set our minds to the blazing of human trails among the inhuman machines.

Industrialism is the one abstraction we're buying now, lock, stock, and barrel. We'll have to be on our toes to keep it from making Yankees of us all.

CHAPTER XII

Of Time:
Past, Present, and Future

As LONG AGO as my boyhood you could buy an Ingersoll
for a dollar. Dollars are more common now, and
so are watches, though not of the dollar brand, but
there are still many people in the South who tell time
by the sun. This is one of the remaining folk characteristics. But more important than how we tell time is what
time tells us, for life comes to us in time, and tells us
whatever it tells us through time.

The chief impression one gets in the South is that
time doesn't tell the Southerner much. Happily or unhappily, he's learning fast, what with three-hundred-
horsepower cars, stoplights, mill whistles, installment
buying, and paydays. I tell my sister-in-law, who's enamored of Northern energy, that so long as you can
ride along the road on a hot July afternoon and see a
Negro stretched out in the blazing sun on the bare floor
of his cabin porch, asleep, the South is safe. I must say
I haven't seen this lately.

Typically, though, the Southerner isn't over-serious
about time. He's not generally aware of the roar of

chariot wheels at his back. He moves, or sits, with a certain looseness, at its best the lithe relaxation of the panther, at its worst the sloth of the pig in the mudhole. The Negro tenant who replied to my criticism of his slowness with the aphorism "There's more fair days than foul, Cap'n" had the Southern attitude toward time.

And he was right. In our climate there are. And I suppose it was the fair days, the rich soil, slavery, and segregation that made him, and the rest of us, feel that way. Slavery, and to a lesser degree segregation, laid heavy emphasis upon what was, and touched but lightly what might be; and thus taught the Negroes—and the poor whites and, indirectly, all of us—to be careless and improvident.

This is not to deny that these institutions made the men who were cut out to be successful planters provident and careful. They had to be. Nor is it to deny the tremendous energy throbbing in Southerners, proved by their westward sweep during the first half of the nineteenth century, their looting of the public domain, their transformation of forests into farms and plantations. Both slaveowners and non-slaveowners engaged in this movement. They seem to have been drawn westward chiefly by a haunting picture of forest-into-plantation, a sort of woods magic in reverse.

But if slavery was perhaps the main force which pushed the plantation westward, how can we say that slavery touched but lightly the future as the source of what might be? The answer is, the dominant drive in the South was forest-into-plantation. This drive envisaged the future as the period in which plantations would be created. It was important, not because it held unknown possibilities, but rather because it held a continuation and extension of the past. The South was a conservative society, first, because it was an agricultural society geared to the rhythm of the seasons and the slow maturing of the crops; second, and more important, because it was a slave society that, so far as slavery was concerned, had to repeat in the future what had been in the past. The condition of the slaves might be ameliorated, and it was; but there was no provision for it to end. The future was to be the past repeated, though improved in detail.

Though the war ended slavery, it did not change the dominant attitude toward time. The future was still envisaged as a repetition of the past. The South simply retreated from the lost line of slavery to the next, and last, line of segregation. It refused—and to some degree still refuses—to see that the forces which had overthrown slavery would certainly in time overthrow segregation. William Archer, commenting in 1910 upon the South's attempt to keep the Negro in a state of serfdom, pointed out this error. "But no more than slavery, I take it, is serfdom permanently possible in a modern democratic state; and in so far as she fails to recognize this, the South is once more trying to put back the hands of time." Because of this error, the future held in the New South practically the same position it had held in the Old: it was a place where we might keep on doing the same things we had done. It was a mere extension of time, not a storehouse of unexplored possibilities.

Questions may be raised. How was, and is, the South different from the North in this regard? Does not

every society project into the future its own past? Did
not the Northern free farmers and mechanics sweep
across their own west, looking for better and bigger
farms, and sites for mills and factories, and water power
and coal: all the things that their hands, guided by their
manipulative, exploitative interests, might convert into
monetary value? This is true. But there was one difference. Being free men, with no burden of unfree men to
maintain and justify, they could continually modify the
raw resources of the future as at the moment they might
wish. If this material modification suggested a modification of the social order, they were free to make it. They
could create, if they wished, from the ground up and
from the inside out.

I think they overdid it. Did too much and did it too
thoughtlessly. They might have asked whether these
changes were demanded by the needs of the machine or
the needs of the human being. They might have observed
that man, somewhat like a plant, establishes certain relations with the world about him and finds life difficult or
impossible if these relations are changed too rapidly or
too radically. But, having said this, I shall have to admit
that the South, projecting into a changeless future its
pattern of race relations, made an error exactly opposite
to that of the North, and one probably just as grievous,
perhaps more so.

An additional factor shaping the mind of the New
South toward time was not present in the Old: our
reverence for the past caused by that past's destruction.
Though the Old South was a traditional society in the
sense that it had an accepted mode of life according to
which men walked in the present as they had walked in

the past, it was still a dynamic society in which men really walked in the present with an eye on the future. It was not looking back to glory; it was creating glory. In its late afternoon, perhaps, Virginia, with tobacco gone west across the mountains and cotton never having come, may have remembered with nostalgia the greater days now gone. But most of the South was on the make, sometimes wildly so.

Then, suddenly, the night came. At the height of its glory the South was destroyed. I should think it was inevitable that the New South in its early days, still faced by its basic problem not ameliorated but intensified, should look backward across the blackened wastes of war and Reconstruction and see the ghost of its own past still standing there upon the hills or in the valleys. The South was, and to a degree still is, bemused by vanished glory. Scattered over the landscape lie ghostly ruins: crumbling churches, lonely columns in green woodlands, and, here and there, the ancient house itself, shining at the far end of an avenue, for all its solid appearance a ghost too, a relic from an earlier world, a shell stranded upon the shore after the spring tides are gone. The mind of the Southerner, beholding these relics, is filled with the pathos of lost time; and, turning his attention to the living and changing institutions about him, he sees them also through pious eyes as crystallized forever. His hearthstone having been uprooted so suddenly and cruelly, he defends as once he defended that hearthstone, not only the customs which grew up around it, but also those, like segregation, of a later date, which he now imagines within that vanished past. If the economic and political order of the South had changed slowly, its social customs would have changed easily with it. But because that order disappeared in a stormy night, the South still clutches to its heart the things it said and did in that lost yesterday.

We have lived like dreamers for ninety years and, like dreamers, fumbled as we picked up the present. We have tried to fit the Negroes into the old pattern, but we fumbled even there, because we have also tried to educate them, and that implies the new. We have tried to bring in industry—and still try, and with increasing effort and success—but at the same time we try to keep "forever unchanged the sacred pattern of life in the South." We are partly right; there is life in the South, and life is sacred; and, because it must exist in patterns, patterns have their sacredness too, as any pious man knows. But we need to ask exactly what is sacred and what made it so, and how we can retain this sacredness as we weave into our life the growing pattern of industrialization. Otherwise, our lives are chaotic, unsatisfactory, and dangerous. It's all right for a dreamer to shift from picture to contradictory picture in his kaleidoscopic dream; it's not all right for men awake; and men have to be awake to live in our world.

Both before and since the Civil War, then, the past has tended to continue itself into the future. The present therefore has tended to be merely the strain of continued work or the relaxation of release from work. The present has tended to be shallow. For human beings vitally alive, however, the present is that creative moment during which the past is warped into the future; and by warped I don't mean twisted out of shape but twisted into such shape as the possibilities suggest. The present is therefore immensely valuable. Though life comes out of the past and looks to the future, its focus is the present; and I think the South, not given to abstractions, realizes this somewhat better than the North. For the man given to abstractions is so dead set on changing things that he has little chance to ponder the value of the thing he is changing or the possible value of the thing he proposes to change it into.

Nevertheless, the South can no longer afford to drift into the future. Indeed, she never could afford it. Yet today she is drifting, her mind filled with ancient dreams, away from her old agricultural order into an increasingly industrial order. With that order will come a new way of life. The South, fearful of *isms*, is accepting in industrialism the father of most of the others. And we are doing it ignorantly. Industry is simply industry to us. That there might be an industrial way of life uncongenial to ours isn't deeply considered. The smoke from the factories is only smoke; it hasn't yet become the powerful genie released from the bottle. But it will. And whether that spirit is good or evil will depend upon the degree to which we understand both it and ourselves.

Industrialism is a high abstraction that, unless modified, will make abstractions of us all. The dyer's hand will be stained by the stuff he works in. Does that mean, then, that in order to protect ourselves and the concrete values we cherish, we must begin, like pseudo-Yankees, to analyze our lives to pieces until, like an onion stripped of all its skins, there's nothing left but a pervasive odor, and that not too pleasant? Must we become the enemy in order to defeat him?

No. But we must take a lesson from him. The

North has analyzed machines and has understood their logic. We must understand the logic of people. We have always claimed to understand people and to be able to get along with them: we stressed manners. We shall have to continue on this path of understanding. We can do this through the science of sociology and through the art of poetry, or, more generally, through intuition. We shall be using in sociology the analytical method of the North, but applied to men, not machines. We are doing this already. What does it mean that in North Carolina there exists now at the state university one of the best schools of sociology in the nation? Just this: that as the South adopts the analytical technique of the North, it applies that technique especially to people, as in sociology, both because its problems have always been people and because it loves its life—its way of life, whatever that is—enough to bring to the study of it some of the best minds of the region.

Does anyone fear that an understanding of our values will destroy them? There is a notion that vagueness itself is valuable, as in sentimental emotions and moonlit scenes. The South is perhaps fond of this notion, being by repute the land of magnolias in the moonlight. I can see no danger here. The vagueness of sentimentality and moonlight is a relatively shallow vagueness. Explain it—away, if you please—and look deeper: the vagueness of life remains. No matter how deep you probe, the vistas still radiate from your latest position and fade in vacancy. No man need lose the mystery of life, no matter how much he analyzes, provided he has it to begin with. There was Einstein, mystic and mathematician. The analyses simply let the sunlight in a little further and push the shadows back. I'm willing to trust Southerners here. I think we have, deep down, a pretty good sense of what life's about, and an unusual sense of its complexity. That's one reason we get confused as we try to live it out in our complex world.

But there is, in addition to analysis and abstraction, another way of understanding. I called it poetry, or, more generally, intuition. This is the immediate perception of value: we know we like this and don't like that. We Southerners have to learn much more to be analytical than to be intuitive. We are by long habit an emotional, impulsive people; we are not an analytical people.

In spite of her poor showing upon the pages of poetry, the South has been poetic: its chief poem is the South. That it is a poem is indicated by the fact that, not only do its own people feel themselves strongly a part of it, but also other people who have never been here have a haunting sense of a strange and somehow desirable land. Generally, the poetry of the South is the poetry of any farming area. For all farming occurs in a vast and harmonious scene, of which the farm is an organic part, supported by influences flowing from that scene, and directing the mind of the farmer down vistaed rows and fields to woods or water or the sundown sky. Farming is also poetic because it follows the rhythmic seasons and the rising and setting of the sun. The mere repetition of action, especially if it is a part of one's livelihood and occurs in a wider, harmonious scene, is in itself poetic. There is also in the South a poetry of the past. It is thus that our childhood is poetic. Like images from the written page, the events rise and shine in memory, and for the same reason as the poetic images. They both re-

veal the life within them: the poem, the poet's life; the
memory, my own. Each person, each society, has some
past, but the South is that region which has pre-eminently a past. It rises beyond the valley of war and
destruction, shining like a Greek temple in a lost eternal
spring. That this is an idealized picture does not matter;
it is the kind of picture which the South, with its history,
had to create.

Much of the poetry of the South has been practical,
didactic. We have created it for purposes of offense or
defense. I do not praise these symbols by listing them;
I merely say that they serve the purpose of practical
poetry and tend to draw the South together against outsiders, or, as regards the white South, against Negroes.
There are, for instance, Southern womanhood, social
equality, mongrelization, "Uncle Tom," the darkey
minstrel, Southern honor, outside interference, damyan-
kee, etc. All these words and images come charged with
emotion; all of them are a practical sort of poetry. Every
country creates some symbols of this type. The South,
having inadvertently set itself against the world, and
sustaining itself, as any conservative society does, largely
by feeling, would naturally create such symbols prolifi-
cally. They are a highly rhetorical poetry; they seek to
move people more toward action than toward understanding. Their weakness is that, like all rhetoric, they
may persuade us to foolish action.

This combined poetical and rhetorical power of the
South can be purified: the rhetoric can be toned down,
the poetry deepened. As the poetry is deepened, we shall
become better aware of what we are. For it is through
the poetic mind that we come to know ourselves. We

can do this today, first, because, being in less danger than
we were, we are in less need of rallying cries and have
more energy left for self-understanding. I know there
are people who will deny that we are in less danger; one
purpose of this book is to show that most of our fears are
baseless. We shall create poetry also because the time
itself leads us in that direction. I do not mean we shall
write more poems—though indeed we shall, and more
novels too. I mean we shall see life more poetically. For
we in the South today are living in an age which suggests
and demands that our life become, in the large sense,
poetic, imaginative. This is because of the nature of our
present, because of the relation of our present to our
future. The weakness of our life has been that the present has been relatively inactive, a mere projection of the
past into the future, more of the same thing. But now,
and increasingly, we shall warp the past into the future.
Safer than ever, wealthier than ever, better educated
than ever, with a new and unpredictable future beckon-
ing to us, and with a great past behind us filled with
human experiences all the way from simple satisfaction
in the morning light to deepest tragedy, we shall find the
present alive in our hands, a mixture of new ideals and
old achievements, suggesting by its very nature that we
become practical poets and warp the desirable old into
the desirable new.

Perhaps for the first time we are beginning to see
the future as a real frontier, more strange and alluring
than any our fathers faced in Mississippi a century and
a quarter ago; for it offers us, not a continuation of the
same life, forest-into-farm, but a chance at a new life,
to be won by us as we realize what we want.

CHAPTER ·XIII·

Diesel at Sundown

WHAT DO WE WANT? What positive ideals do we have
which are edging out the old negative wish to keep
things unchanged and the Negro in his place? In the
millrace of the present—rat race for so many—the future belongs to those who can imagine it; those who
only clutch the past are doomed. What future, different
from our past, can we with our past imagine and desire?

To raise such questions is to assume the importance
of interests and ideals. No one will question the importance of interests; but as I have called my uncle a
true Southerner when he said "Ideals are a sin, Alice; we
should love God," perhaps I should defend the inclusion
of ideals as factors in the future of the South. Three
years ago, in the wake of the Supreme Court's decision,
a later-generation kinsman of that uncle spoke a milder
piece: "Idealists are all right in their place, but this is a
job for practical men." From this point of view, ideals
are no longer sinful, but neither are they of particular
virtue. Or perhaps they are if they are the right ideals.
For on the same occasion another speaker, warning his
hearers that segregation might be lost, declared that
where there is no vision the people perish. Here the
vision—the ideal—was held necessary to salvation.

The point of this is that the South does move, however slowly, into the modern world, where all things are subject to change; and the basic questions become *how?* and *to what degree?* Even my uncle, conservative though he was, did not carry the whole past with him; that is impossible. He chose, according to his—perhaps unrecognized—ideals, the things he would cherish. So do we today. We have a range of choice, however, not open to him in the limited South of the 1900's. Ideals and interests, long smothered by harsh conditions, today reappear and shape the social order.

The South has often complained of outside interference. This complaint is probably unrealistic. From the beginning the South willed to be a part of the interdependent modern world, and is therefore properly subject to the criticism of that world. But more to the point here is the implication that if we were free from outside interference we should be free. We shall be free only as we understand what we want and adopt the proper measures for its attainment. It isn't primarily a question of what the South should do; it's primarily a question of what the South wants to do. And this is where self-knowledge comes in. It isn't ideals themselves that are wrong; all men advance under the pressure of circumstances and the lure of ideals; what is wrong is the wrong ideals, or a confusion of ideals. If the ideals that the world suggests are not right for us, what ideals are right? The function of thought, as Schweitzer says, is to determine the ideals that illumine actuality. Such ideals have compelling power. What are the basic, the bedrock ideals of the South? What are the fundamental desires that move us, and what chance have they in the modern world?

Most evident is our long-continued and deepening urge to industrialize our economy. As we achieve this desire, the wall of segregation crumbles. For technology knows nothing of race, regardless of how important it may seem to certain industrialists who seek a short-term gain by pitting machine operatives against one another. In the long run these operatives catch on and, uniting across racial and other lines, demand a fair share in the profits they help to create. This is what is happening now, even in the South, in the ranks of the CIO. This, at least in our democratic climate, is inevitable.

Harry Ashmore, editor of the *Arkansas Gazette*, has recently said: "Southern leaders who are working, with marked success, to industrialize the region, are undermining the system of segregation so many of them passionately defend."

Unfortunately, the machine is as ignorant of people as it is of race. Left to itself, it produces goods. As much as the South needs goods, the kindly, human South does not want goods at the price of basic values. This raises a complex problem, and it is not surprising that we have been, and still are, confused. But we are approaching the time when both our needs and our resources indicate that much of this confusion will be cleared up.

Walter Hines Page, devoted Southerner but honest critic of the South, suggested this problem as early as 1902: "If you are determined to find a problem," he wrote, "you may reflect on this: how in the march of industrialism these qualities of hospitality and leisure may be retained in the habits of these people; and how they may be transplanted to corresponding towns in other parts of the Union. For the practice of kindliness and of restfulness is not a trick, not a mere fashion or tradition: it is a quality of the blood, a touch of nature that would redeem the unlovely wastes of much more prosperous and better informed society."

Our basic trouble is, we don't know what we want. We are pioneers who are changing the face of the country without any clear picture of what is to replace the wilderness. By the grace of water power, and now of electricity, we dot our landscape with mills, lured by nothing more solid than a rise in the standard of living. For the moment, this is sufficient. But we know on good authority that man does not live by bread alone, but by a dream, a vision, a picture of something he hopes to accomplish or of something he intends to defend.

If any people in the world should know this, we should. For what is our life but a congeries of significant pictures and phrases, the most universal being the very words "The South"? That includes all the others, from mint juleps to white supremacy. They have been the rallying cries that have made the South solid, for enjoyment or defense.

I think it has been too solid. The South thinks so too, or at least acts that way. For in adopting the mode of production of the Western world she will inevitably become more like the Western world. She will find lines of interest crossing her borders more and more often, influences emanating from her to the world and flowing from the world back upon her. Fortunately, though provincial, the South has never been isolationist. She is upset now, especially her white citizens, partly because she fears she is being misunderstood. As she adopts the common mode of production, she can give and take freely and forget the old need to be solid in the lasting need to be herself, true to the best she has learned.

What is the best she has learned? What dream is there more real than the offered tons of production and cash income? If it is to attract us, it must suggest in terms of the future the best of the past.

But, you say, if we are changing from an agrarian to an industrial order, all we have to do is adopt the industrial ideal. What is the industrial ideal? It has never been stated. Sheer production? Industrialism is one of those really dangerous *isms* whose danger lies chiefly in the fact that it so fascinates us—indeed, charms us— with the means of production that we fail to inquire as to the ends. We produce machines so cunning that, staring at them, we are hypnotized and begin to imitate their actions.

Industrialism tends to depersonalize, to dehumanize, to mechanize the men who operate it. Not only the men who run the machines, but the men who run these men, the men who produce for the machines, and the men who consume the machine products—that is, all of us. For the machines have a logic of their own, and if you turn them loose, they will drag persons wildly along with them.

The essential problem here is the taming of power; and, because the power comes from nature, it is the humanization of nature. The fission of the atom is the best illustration. This is almost the final achievement— to date—of the analytical, co-operative mind of man. We have analyzed matter away, abstracting from the solid earth layer by layer until only the mathematical equation remains. We have produced machines that will follow our mathematics into the atom itself and turn loose the raw power at its core; and we have turned it loose. We have gone one step further and learned to fuse atoms, an action that results in the release of even more astounding power. We have turned that loose too. And, now, what are we going to do? We have released the genie from the bottle, and he mushrooms against the sky. More prosaically, we have caught a bear by the tail.

Cave men tried to avoid bears: nature was something to keep away from. Later on, men began to corral them: nature was something to be controlled. But yesterday we raised such a bear as we had never dreamed of, and today we have him by the tail, unable to turn him loose or tame him. We have raised in what may be its final form the problem of the humanization of nature.

But what has this to do with the South? Well, isn't the South in the world? Isn't the world in the South? Where is Oak Ridge? And where is the Savannah River Project? Ninety miles as the crow flies southwesterly from where I sit, and the prevailing winds blow from that direction. The bear is in South Carolina. Industrialization grows among us, and we don't know any better than anyone else how to control it. Specifically, we don't know what we want it to do.

More than most people, however, we have the means of finding out. It isn't simply that at this critical point in our development we naturally desire to find out; we have also the resources to find out. Within our own not distant past lies the experience that, if understood, will show us what, under the coming industrial order, we want.

The antebellum South was a semi-feudal society; it

was therefore a semi-medieval society. Medieval society rested upon the concept of status, or place. With the coming of the modern world, this concept was replaced by free contract: every member of society, now no longer both constrained and supported within a fixed place, could contract for himself any place he could persuade society to give him. The entire modern productive system is based upon this. The swift advance of the modern world is connected with it, as is also the insecurity of modern man. The South, however, longer than the rest of the Western world, has maintained some vestige of status and the attendant security, and has refused to adopt completely free contract, freedom, and the attendant insecurity.

It retains this sense because it's close to feudalism. Indeed, many feudal attitudes linger on, awkward and distorted, on the great cotton plantations. The rest of the nation, having been modern so long, has largely forgotten it. Yet now, not knowing what it's looking for, it's looking for it again. This is the meaning of the quest for security. Many people think of this as a quest for material security. It's more than this, and the South knows it, even though she doesn't know she knows it. The South has the resources to explain what modern society is really seeking, and perhaps how this may be attained in an industrial order.

As yet, the South isn't deeply concerned to find the spiritual security sought by modern man, because she hasn't really lost it. But she will lose it if she merely grabs the offered factories and plants them in the fields. What do we want of the factories? What do we wish to save, what can we save, from our old life? What picture, what phrase, may sum up what we want, may suggest an achievable dream, in the realization of which our hands may be busy? It's far too late now to dream of pillared piazzas.

If I really knew, I should write the new "Dixie." There sticks in my mind, however, an image and a phrase: "the diesel at sundown." I saw it recently as I was driving home. One of those big ten- to twenty-ton jobs passed me and, swinging into the lane ahead, loomed against the sundown sky. It wasn't speeding, it was just rolling easy, the pale smoke drifting from the stack. As I watched it, there came to me the words: "the diesel going home at sundown," and, with the words and with a shock of delighted surprise, a remembered picture, seen many times in the quiet countryside, a heritage of our Western past, immortalized by the Latin poets two thousand years ago: the smoke rising from the peasant's hut at evening. It was the diesel's smoke against the sundown which reminded me of the country picture and the Latin poets, and the shock of delight was due to the fact that these two dissimilar things had so fused in my mind, that the smoke of the diesel rose from the peasant's hut and the diesel itself at sundown was some-how going home.

Both pictures suggest the taming of nature. The Roman peasant, by the help of Prometheus, had captured the fire from heaven and set it to boiling the pot upon his hearth and to warming himself and his family in the cool evening and the chilly night. The Romans also used this fire for productive processes outside the home; but it was reserved for modern man to extend and rationalize this use. Thus, the fire from heaven burns now primarily in factories and in engines of various kinds—as in the throbbing heart of the diesel that passed me at sundown. It was the drift of smoke from the stack, the relaxed breath of power under the hood which suggested the tamed warmth within the peasant's cottage.

But the smoke from the cottage was the sign of a fire that, though seized from nature, maintained a close relation to nature, burning most in winter and at evening, in the rhythm of the seasons and the hours, at sunrise, and noon, and sundown. But what had the smoke from the diesel to do with sundown? I merely happened to see it against that backdrop. To the diesel sundown meant nothing, nor midnight, nor rain, nor any other creature. Fifteen minutes after sundown the lights would come on, first the dimmers and then the driving lights, and within its own daylight the diesel would roll through the night. The fires that once we had built upon hearths at stated times in the rhythm of nature we now kept roaring day and night, winter and summer. We who had learned to work by daylight and the bright summer days, and to rest in the darkness of night or of winter, now worked in shifts around the mechanical clock and the calendar year.

The peasant's fire reminded him that he still belonged to the world of nature, from which he had seized it. Though its master, he was also its youngest brother. Thus, he humanized nature without denaturalizing himself. But we control the natural fires so completely that they hardly remind us of nature any more: we floodlight the night and air-condition the seasons. By such control we denaturalize ourselves; and, though in the intense conditions of modern life we become nationals of this country or that and find thereby some status, we lose the far more fundamental sense of being citizens of a heaven-surrounded earth. As the fires we control become stronger and more pervasive, we find our ties with nature growing increasingly tenuous. We become aliens in a world in which we had once been at home.

When we set the fire outside the home, we began to dehumanize it. We have now let it run so far that we have frightened the night away and challenged the noon-day sun, and so have denaturalized ourselves. And the questions arise: How shall we be at home with this power which we have torn from the roots of the world? How shall we bring it back to leash? How shall we find again something of the old rhythm, the joyful brightness of the day, and the restful solace of the night? In brief, how shall we bring the diesel home?

In minor ways we tame this fire now. We still live in homes, even though many of them are apartments, and still use the ancient fire to light us and warm us and cook our food and, recently, run our do-it-yourself machines. Is not this more effective than what the peasant did? In a sense, yes. We get far more fire than he did, and with far less effort—direct effort, that is. We press a button and the heat comes on; the peasant laboriously cut wood and dragged it in and fanned the embers. The difference is—and it is essential—he tamed the fire himself; we press a button. And he kept it tame—except when it overleaped its bounds and burned down his hut. When I sit before an open fire, it seems marvelous that men should build a house and then in the middle of it build a roaring fire. The fires that warm our truly modern houses are tamer and more effective than this, but it is not we who have tamed them. The Promethean power which once they stirred in us, the knowledge that we had bridled and were now handling the horses of the sun, has faded from our spirits. Though they are faithful most of the time, we know deep down that they were driven to our doors by strangers, and that if those strangers should fail us we should be back in the cold without even the flint and steel.

The ironic fact is that we have harnessed as never before these fiery horses, but through controls so intricate that, though every man has his hand upon the reins, no man can really believe it, while at the same time every man fears that some man somewhere may slip the bridles and let the wild stallions loose.

If the diesel at sundown had been running toward the driver's home as to its stall, if the driver's children had come out to greet their father and this lumbering beast of burden, and if from that home and stall the driver had set forth again at dawn for another day-long foray into the countryside, that would have been an old and human pattern. The central fire would have been on the hearth, and from this fire the diesel would run forth day after day, and night after night return to it. In such a pattern nature would be humanized and man not denaturalized, spiritual relationships would exist within physical relationships, and livelihood and life might be one.

In such situations there is security. For security obtains where physical interdependence is accompanied by love. This might be the situation if the diesel were really going home. We know, however, that it's not; that was a pretty picture and nothing more.

I'm not arguing against the industrial revolution; I'm merely indicating an unforeseen and unfortunate effect, and wondering how we can counteract it.

There is a physical way to bring the factory and the home closer together. Unfortunately, it suggests the mill village of unhappy memory. That village, however, was purely an affair of convenience. The mill workers had to live somewhere; poor transportation facilities made it impossible for them to live far away. The mill-owner, therefore, threw up a village just outside the mill and stuck the people in it. He thereby had the workers not only at hand but also under his thumb. The mill village in the South was only a replica, in industry, of the cotton plantation: the mill-owner was the plantation master, and the people were his people. Even this, in the hard 1880's, was a blessing. As for the evils, they do not inhere in the village itself.

Suppose factory-ownership not so monolithic as at present, with a much wider financial interest among the employees; suppose that homes, schools, nurseries, churches, clubs, and park-like areas are grouped about the factory; suppose consistent efforts on the part of management to strengthen instead of weaken the ties between livelihood and life, between factory and home. You would have the life of the home and the life of the factory crossing and influencing each other, and men would know better what they were working for because they would have it generally in view. For most of us only know the meaning of our lives as we see them; and most of us today, seldom seeing our lives as a whole, means and ends together, seldom know what we're doing.

Or suppose an extension of what we often have at present, especially in the South: the factory set in the open country or beside a village; the workers settled within that countryside in an area stretching for miles, in homes with gardens and perhaps small farms. Ideally, the factory would stand upon a hill near the center of the landscape and would be visible from most places within the circle. Thus the workers would be able to view from their homes the source of their livelihood, and from the factory their homes, where their women and children would be waiting.

There is one flaw in this picture: it is too reminiscent of the cathedral of the Middle Ages. The factory begins to look like a church. As, according to William H. Whyte, Jr., in *The Organization Man*, the executive organization behind the factory begins to look like a religious brotherhood. To put the factory at the center of the landscape seems to set livelihood at the heart of life. Livelihood is basic to life and if detached from life, as we have detached it, will become the end of life instead of its beginning. To set the factory on a hill overlooking the homes of the workers is to suggest that we're working for the factory—which, unfortunately, is already too true: capital employing labor, things employing men. In any sensible view, the factory exists for the home; the picture we have imagined hardly suggests this.

Whether this picture is satisfactory or not, we live by pictures. Modern life is poor because it lacks significant pictures. Southern life is confused because it cherishes unreal pictures.

But perhaps there are other ways of establishing a closer connection between our jobs and our lives, or closing the rifts within us, and thus making of us solid and integrated men. Barring world disaster, we shall not bring the factory back into the home. If it is to remain outside, what, beyond the suggestions already made, can be done to make it homelike?

I can hear the efficiency experts snorting. Let them snort. They're the boys who split the atom and threw the tortured creature in my lap. That wasn't so bright.

What, then, is homelike? Well, what is home? The old adage is solid enough: home is a castle. At the other extreme is that nice definition of Frost's: "something you somehow haven't to deserve," a gift, a bit of God's grace. Both these statements say the same thing: home is where you are secure, protected physically, as by the walls of a castle, spiritually by the gift of your place, or status, there. In this ideal situation the physical and the spiritual are intertwined.

It seems impossible to duplicate in the factory this situation. How close can we come to it, and by what means? Physical security is obtained there, first, through safety devices; modern industry does this increasingly. It is also obtained through the union, which secures good jobs and wages. This second type of security passes over into the spiritual; but spiritual security is more than this. It is the gift of status in the group, and depends upon the recognition, by the group and by society, that each man holds a place, not merely by will and skill, but by the desire of all. He is in his job as a free man, but he is also there because society wants him to be there, recognizes his right to be there, and makes it known in various ways.

This probably means some sort of co-operative venture. The workers must be drawn more closely into both the conduct and the ownership of business. A man must feel that his place is his own, but partly by free gift of the others: something that in some sense he hasn't to deserve. How can he feel this about a mere wage or salary job? He must have some ownership in it. It was this the sitdown-strikers were really contending for in 1937: they felt they had an equity in the machines they had been operating. Essentially, and historically, they were right. But they made the mistake of sitting down beside idle machines.

If it be objected that bringing the workers into a larger ownership will make management thereby more difficult and perhaps even inefficient, one could admit the possibility and still defend the wisdom of the move by pointing out, as we have proved concerning political democracy, that though such democracy may be in the short run inefficient, in the long run it reveals both endurance and ability to pack a wallop. Actually, one need not admit the possible retardation of industry through a more extended productive democracy; for advanced industries, seeking efficiency, are already decentralizing responsibility from top management down to the worker in the ranks.

The basic difficulty of these suggestions is that we are trying here to bring together the virtues of a mobile society of free contract and a stratified society of status. Our problem is: how to have a place in society without being frozen in that place? We shall have either to discover the static within the dynamic or the dynamic within the static, or find some more basic term that includes them both.

This is the kind of problem we face, especially in

the South, where we are riding the tide of industrialism while still aware of the virtues of an older way of life. We should be indeed foolish if we did not attempt to preserve these virtues: life is not so generous as to warrant discarding the treasures it has given. With enough thought we might retain them. First, because they are clear in our minds when we ponder them. Second, because the industrial pattern has not yet crystallized into the stark capital-versus-labor conflict, and may therefore be more easily shaped to some happier form.

All this seems highly theoretical. But I remember a recent conversation between two of my friends regarding production difficulties in a South Carolina factory. One of them said the trouble was simply wages. Up the wages by thirty-seven cents an hour, to the Northern level, and satisfactory production would follow. Said the other, a Catholic priest who serves as a labor-management consultant: "No, the manager doesn't know his men. He's driving them too hard. They want time for neighborly comments, like 'How's that kid getting on?' and 'Say, let's go fishing Saturday.' If he would let up on the pressure, the production would rise. He's dealing with Southern countrymen."

The Old South was home, with all its personal meanings. The new South is power, summed up by the diesel. What we're looking for is what, most happily, I saw: the diesel at sundown, rolling home. For sundown is ideally what Sappho said it was—the time that brings all things home, even diesels.

What has this to do with race relations in the South? It underlies them. We permitted the unhappy events of Reconstruction to distract us from the basic problem of production and to confuse us with the pseudo-problem of race. We have thus approached industrialism with backward glance, and with one hand thrust behind us pushing the Negro down. As a consequence, we haven't been able even to raise the standard of living as we should have, and as for facing the vital problem of industrialism, we hardly know it exists. Race seemed the problem in 1876; if I had been there, doubtless I should have ridden red-shirted with Hampton. But now, awakening from that nightmare, we begin to see the real problem, which is also the problem of the industrial West and the industrializing East. As we tackle it, racial problems will tend to solve themselves, and we shall give to a world wherein hungry and humiliated people demand machines and equality a vision both of plenty and of peace, peace between the races and within ourselves.

It is the strength of a conservative society that it carries the past with it; it is its weakness that it carries too much. It is the strength of the South that, though conservative, it has always had a frontier to strain and jar the old pattern. Within the last century that frontier has been overwhelming, and, faced with heart-breaking economic and social demands, we have let the pioneering instinct lie frustrated and festering within us. Happily, those days are either gone or going. Once again the old sense of something hid behind the ranges, of "gold in them thar hills," rises within us. Only, this time the mountains to be crossed are the mountains of the mind, and the gold to be found is the essential gold of happy human relations and the happy heart.

Let's bring the diesel home!

CHAPTER ·XIV·

"Pioneers, O Pioneers"

THERE IS ANOTHER FORCE in the South, within us and
beyond us, cracking old patterns and creating new
ones. This is the frontier and the pioneer spirit it
arouses.

The South has always had a frontier; through most
of the past century, too much frontier. Men halted at
the challenge and dug in where they were. The earlier
pioneering spirit was frustrated. The task was too great
for our resources, and we crouched along the edges of
despair. But we have now come to happier times. Has
the challenge grown less than in the nineties? On the
contrary. Then we faced a racial problem in the South
(the North having largely withdrawn); now we face it
in the world. Why do we not despair, then? Because our
resources have grown faster than the challenge. It is our
momentary misfortune that we are not yet clearly aware
of these resources.

Like all Americans, we have a frontier tradition.
With eagerness, even impetuosity, we overran our west
of the early nineteenth century. The lust for virgin lands
was in our blood. When my father pulled up stakes in
1906 and left cleared land for almost solid woods, he was
repeating, though in a limited way, the pioneering ges-

ture; and the immediate environment in which we settled was almost as raw as Alabama a hundred years before.

The great, settled plantations of the Old South were relatively few. For the region as a whole, they were ideals to be striven for, not accomplishments already attained. Captain Basil Hall, the English traveler who visited the South in 1827–8, noticed that, except in race relations, Southerners, like all Americans, subjected everything to "one unceasing round of crude alterations— adopted as soon as suggested." William Gregg, the "Father of Southern Cotton Manufacturing," complained in 1845 that South Carolinians were too quick to change, too rootless, hesitating to build even a comfortable dwelling-house, "Lest the spirit of emigration deprive [them] of its use"; ready to abandon soil still fertile "in search of a country affording new and better lands." Yet, led by such men as Edmund Ruffin of Virginia, Southerners were pioneers among Americans in the use of manures and fertilizers for rebuilding worn-out soils. Only in two areas was the South typically unadventurous: manufacturing and social relationships. It was an agrarian society, supported by slave labor, and pursuing an aristocratic ideal. For the rest, we were Americans.

But, unlike other Americans, we have had the pioneering drive pretty well dammed up in us now for ninety years. If it has curdled, if frustrations have bred aggressions, what does one expect? We should have been less than ourselves if we had accepted complacently the defeats we have suffered since 1860.

Consider where the war left us. The entire South

had become a frontier again. First, a physical frontier—not, this time, unbroken forest, but twisted rails, blown bridges, blackened ruins, and tools and machines worn out or destroyed. We had faced the primeval forest with the best axes of that time; we faced these ruins with almost empty hands. The war had taught us to make machines like Yankees, but they had been perforce war machines—mainly guns—and the war itself had left the foundries smoking ruins. The violence that swept the South, and that still to some degree exists—the personal fights, the murders, and the lynchings—was partly frontier violence: the violence of the lonely countryside, an uprooted social order, few officers of the law. Such violence, though not so much of it, had existed in the South before the war. It continued now on a wider scale, the product both of the new physical frontier and of the unsettled social area where whites and Negroes met.

For this was the second frontier we faced, and this is the frontier we have found it hardest to settle. The war dissolved the old relation between whites and Negroes and left in its place an unsettled area, a social frontier, in the settlement of which we are still engaged.

When a people settles a physical frontier, it is usually agreed as to the means and ends of settlement. The group brings its own social and political ideals with it, and, though these may be roughly handled in the early years, men soon establish approximations of the old forms of law. The post-war South, however, could not agree on the social form to be housed in the physical structure, itself not yet rebuilt. Even the white South did not agree; it felt, however, so desperately the need for agreement that it whipped all whites into line. Certainly the Negroes did not agree with the whites. Whatever rights and privileges they really wanted, it is certain they didn't want the same things the whites wanted for them. Finally, the nation did not agree: did not agree with itself, for the humanitarians among the Republican Radicals did not want what the businessmen wanted; more important, did not agree with the white South.

Contrast this situation with the other frontier efforts of our history. We found the Indians occupying the land. Here and there a man like William Penn dealt honestly with them. By and large, however, the settlers simply killed them or pushed them westward. When upon one occasion the nation tried, through the Supreme Court, to defend against Georgia the treaty rights of the Cherokees, President Jackson would not sustain the Court, and the Georgians had their way.

After the Civil War, however, every attempt to settle the Negro-white frontier had to be considered in the light of the reaction in Washington. Would the nation permit it? The nation had never really defended the Indians; from 1861 to 1865 it had poured out blood and treasure for the Negroes. No matter what the North began the war for, its most striking immediate effect was the freeing of the slaves; and the North would have been less than human if it had not concluded that it had fought the war in order to free the slaves. Therefore it had to defend them. As their presence in this new frontier South was far more serious for the South than the presence of the Indians had ever been for the American settlers, the problem raised by the attitude of the nation must have seemed to the white South almost insoluble. To make it even harder, the South faced the problem with no faith that it could be settled according to Northern demands. Slavery had held on until forcibly destroyed partly because Southerners had been unable to imagine a workable order that would include the freed Negroes. By 1865 the South had had enough of war; she surely did not want to fight the North again, nor did she want Federal troops quartered upon her. Yet at every step she took toward the only kind of settlement she could imagine, something on the antebellum order, she had to weigh the chance of the nation's opposition and reprisal.

But, even in the light of these difficulties, if the physical resettlement could have succeeded and have continued to succeed, the South could have faced the problem of racial settlement with a calmer and more effective mind. But what happened? After a burst of splendor, with cotton bringing from fifty cents to a dollar a pound, the world's markets were flooded, the price swung downward, and from 1875 to 1900 kept dropping till it reached five cents. Once the respected king, cotton was now the tyrant, from whose clutches the productive system prevented men from escaping, and within whose clutches they could hardly survive. They were frustrated economically by the physical frontier, spiritually by the racial. The frontier situation, which, ideally, should have called out again the American spirit within them, had become so complex, so apparently insoluble, that its effect turned inward, to curdle unexpressed, and to erupt in greater violence than the South at peace had ever known.

So frustrated were the whites by the difficulty and complexity of this dual frontier that they decided, in

effect, not to settle its racial aspect but to block it off
and leave it there forever. This they did by segregation
and disfranchisement. They called it a settlement; with
their conscious minds most of them probably thought
it was, though here and there a man with a tough pioneer
spirit spoke out and said that nothing had been settled
at all. Actually, by these regulations the Negroes were
pushed further away than ever and became an increasingly unknown quantity. By 1900 the form of settlement
had been established. The unsettled racial frontier was
nominally gone. Around the Negroes a sharp line had
been drawn, and within this magic circle they were to
remain, unknown, unassimilated, and supposedly unas-
similable. Here, for once, the melting-pot was supposed
not to melt.

But it stayed hot. The peace thus established was
an unquiet peace. White men told themselves that now,
with the Negro safely encircled, the South could go
about its business. It didn't work out that way, and it
couldn't have. Henceforth, nothing could be said or
done without relating it to the Negro question. We
didn't admit this, of course; but the fact remains that
the Negro has been the dominant force in Southern
politics and life since 1865. Though the problem has been
out of sight, its shadow has remained to darken our
minds and dampen our spirits. In such a mood we could
not see the future, with its widening horizons.

But now, under the weight of time and the wills of
countless men, ourselves included, the encircling wall of
segregation is crumbling. The Negro problem—an abstraction to be feared if any abstraction should be—is
fading, and the Negro as a human being is taking its

place. Our fears are fading too with our ignorance and our poverty, and we, especially the youthful among us, are ready to face the frontiers of our time.

They are essentially frontiers of the mind. Said another South Carolinian, Ben Robertson, in 1942: "In the South, I have known that from our time on, we would be obliged to find what it is we look for within ourselves. . . . It is ourselves now that we must settle." This is exactly what Thoreau said a hundred years ago to New England, then rushing wildly into industrialism. Here in the South these inner frontiers have long invited our attention, but it is only in recent years that we have begun to accumulate the material and spiritual resources that both make us aware of them and give us some hope of settling them. What we are chiefly concerned with is the new technological horizon and the new racial horizon. Up to the present we have faced the technological horizon mainly as a physical frontier, and the racial horizon, not as a true frontier of any kind, not as an open land, but as a blank wall, an insoluble problem, and one therefore of no real interest.

As for the technological horizon, the industrial frontier, if we should become absorbed in its real problems, the racial frontier might well settle itself. But as we have in the settlement of this frontier a lever to lift the world, it might be well to consider it separately.

The racial frontier now encircles the world and demands a settlement. Throughout the modern imperialistic period the white race has held toward the colored races essentially the same attitude that the white race in the South has held toward the Negroes here, that of assumed superior to inferior, and has practiced the discrimination and exploitation attached thereto. During this period no true social frontier existed between the races. The relative positions were at least superficially accepted; the whites kept the superior places, the colored peoples the inferior. But mankind now, even in Africa, is on the march, the old interracial ties are breaking, and in place of that settlement, however uneasy it may have been, there exist a present unsettlement and a growing need for the white and colored races to come to some agreement. For the situation is fluid, indeed revolutionary, and, like any true frontier, challenges those who live alongside it to face it and from its wildness effect a satisfactory—if possible, a profitable—settlement.

Such a frontier is a far more serious challenge than the old physical frontiers. Then we merely pushed forward through nature, absorbing or driving the natives before us. Now the natives too are pioneering; their will is at least equal to ours in the choice of the settlement to be made. Where, once, force and mechanical skill were enough, now these tools are largely outmoded, and in their place we must use diplomacy, the old Southern skill of manners. These new frontiers are asking the South simply to be itself and bring to their settlement its best resources.

Even better than that, these frontiers lie not only across the seas and thus inaccessible to most of us, but also next door, down the street or down the road. Here are the racial frontiers of the world, stretching from Bishopville, South Carolina, to Benares, India. In the former town, in the winter of 1949, a white bridge-builder, invited into a Negro home to warm, saw on the wall a portrait of Mahatma Gandhi. The South is a pilot plant, set up under fortunate circumstances, where the white and colored races can learn how to settle the frontier that now divides them. Here, more easily than anywhere else, the job can be successfully done. Those who are Calvinists might well believe that the South, like Queen Esther, has come to the kingdom for such a time as this.

For here are the Negroes living all around us, of whom we say in our complacent moments we understand them, but of whom we also say, in pessimistic vein, nobody understands them. They, too, looking across at us, shake their heads and mutter: *White folks is white folks.* Yet we are not to them the mystery they are to us. They had to understand us; we could overlook them. Consequently, for most whites the Negroes have existed in the South like patches of deep woods darkening a sunny landscape. We accepted the woods, avoided it, and lived on our open acres. But now it has become necessary to settle that forest. Thus, from being an area "dull, dark and soundless," clothed in perpetual autumn, it has become for us a true frontier. Though still unknown, it is now ready to yield its valuable secrets to those who venture therein. The urgency of the times forces us to venture. It would have been better if the white people of the South, through native stoutness of heart, had accepted long ago the challenge of this unknown forest and, instead of fencing it off, had, in the spirit of true pioneers, breached its borders and spread throughout its expanse the light of common aims and efforts. In brief, had settled it. But, being too hard-pressed by misfortune and the very burden of existence, we failed to do this. We waited until the pressure of events thrust us stumbling across the border into that unknown land. So, today, we are racial adventurers—not of the first water perhaps, but adventurers still. The future has again assumed its true business: it has become dangerous and challenging; and, for better or worse, we are being loosed from the past and pushed into the future.

It is too late now to live by the past. The Maginot Line is lost; the wall of segregation crumbling; the god of the wall departing. It was a sad day for the South when she enthroned a god upon the wall and made of segregation a sacred thing. To become the people of the wall! I search my heart, but cannot find it in me. Nor in my happy, full-bosomed mother; less in my pioneering father; least of all, the further back I go, in that gray-bearded fighter, the old Confederate who, at eighty, longed still for time to see "the whole thing wound up." And far behind him, towering above him, there looms against the sky the ancient Southern god, the pillar of fire by night and of cloud by day, forever leading us out of the wilderness into the Promised Land.

For we are not simply being pushed into the future; we are also going of our own free will. Even as long ago as 1909, when we had just accepted formally the job of keeping the Negro down, a wise Southerner, Edgar Gardner Murphy, recognized the pioneering spirit of the South. "We are too busy," he said, "too much interested in other things, too eager for larger enterprises and freer minds, to be consumingly engaged in the business of keeping someone down. The thing, moreover, is impossible. Not only is the Negro growing stronger, but the whole world will daily add to his strength in direct proportion to the repression which he suffers." Five years after Murphy spoke, a shot rang out at Sarajevo, the modern political revolution began, the colored peoples of the world turned in their sleep, and the world racial frontier began to take form.

Thus, at almost the same moment the pioneer spirit was stirring, however faintly, in the South and the world situation was shaping into such a challenge as we had never known. Fifty years have now passed, time and happier local conditions have little by little removed many of our Southern frustrations, the world challenge whose imminent dawn Murphy but faintly discerned now dominates the eastern sky, and both from that challenge and from the native drive within us we recapture the spirit of our pioneering fathers, who out of raw forests built commonwealths, and who now challenge us to build upon the land they thus subdued a true and democratic settlement.

They do not challenge us to do the things they did. The great forests are gone, the great cities rising. To each generation its own duties. They challenge us to face, with the devoted courage of our tradition and such vision as we can command, the duties of today.

These duties begin at our doors and encircle the world. As Ben L. Smith, superintendent of the Greensboro, North Carolina, schools, said recently: "The hour of desegregation has struck, and it is the position of leadership in the world which the U.S. has taken which makes it inevitable."

But, even beyond the pioneering tradition of the South, the pioneer spirit—like love, its other name, indeed—never completely fails. It rises perennially in the human heart. It is the eternal lure of novelty. With us, moreover, this spirit lies very close to the surface, dammed up and frustrated by a mere ninety years, rising now to the challenge of the unsettled and the wild. This is the essential appeal of the frontier: in contrast to the settlements, it is the land of the wild, where unknown forces are waiting to be harnessed, unknown dangers to prove one's manhood. "Now, God be thanked who has matched us with this hour," cried Rupert Brooke, entering the wild frontier of 1914. We've had enough of the frontier of war; our job is the frontier of peace. Life is at least not boring any more, as it had been to Brooke in what seem to me now those halcyon days before 1914 but what seemed to him then a heavy complacency. Every day for us is a bringer of new things, and our grandfathers' grandsons rise to greet the unseen with a cheer.

For, despite the tragic drama of her history, the South is cheerful. Or because of it. He who has had great reverses takes reverses lightly. If life becomes hard enough, it may become easy. The Old South liked to think of itself as a Greek state, a select aristocracy upheld by slavery, and indeed its pillared mansions recall the Greek temples. But most of all the arc of its life was Greek, both in its splendor and in its tragic end. Greek, too, in its inner spirit: overweening pride, *hubris*.

But, regardless of the tragic drama the South enacted, the Southerner has never taken life too seriously. Neither climate nor conscience demanded it. On the contrary, the material rewards of great daring encouraged the gambler in him. He couldn't keep his eye on a job. Life wasn't a business; it was at best an adventure, at worst, luck. The slaves were improvident and, whether in spite of their fate or because of it, gay. They may have struck the deepest human chords in their melancholy spirituals, making, as men do, their sweetest songs from saddest thought; but most of their music is joyful, even rollicking. The white South has not heard these songs entirely in vain.

With this lightness of heart, with this devil-may-care touch of the cavalier, not only are we of the South fitted by inheritance to pioneer, but we are also better fitted than most men to do the social pioneering the day demands. We have the grand tool of manners. But, even beyond that, we have stored within us—I shall not say an unruffled pool of peace, for no man who lives in our troubled world but has his heart ruffled by the tornadoes sweeping the globe. But I will say that we in the South have in our relaxation, our ease, our friendliness, a peace which we maintain not simply because it is good for business, but because it is good. I grant that it too quickly breaks into violence; I grant we need to undergird our manners with justice and the passion for justice. But we have reserved in our lives a place for peace and quiet and neighborliness; and from this place, as small and insecure as it is, we may move outward upon great adventures.

For adventure—all adventure, but certainly into such social frontiers as challenge us now—is largely the product of peace. We are confused in this matter. We think of adventure as being connected with violence and war. That's what poor Brooke thought; perhaps he died too young ever to realize his mistake. Violence and war lead not to adventure but to its opposite, boredom. The adventuring spirit, which is essentially the spirit of the pioneer, is best suggested by those romances of the Middle Ages where the knight rides forth into a world, for all its evils and dangers, essentially good, a world that offers great prizes to the man who accepts its challenge.

I am not recommending the re-establishment of the Southern tournaments. They were mainly amusing. Except, perhaps, for one thing: the Southern knight rode to honor some fair lady. I'm perfectly willing for the fair lady to climb down from her pedestal and stretch her legs; she's doing it anyhow. But the medieval knight himself rode for personal reasons and lived in a personal world. This the South remembers, and this it should never forget.

Adventure, then, occurs in a world deeply at peace and interested in persons. I know of no better way to suggest the relation between adventure and peace than to recount an incident of my boyhood. I think it was a composite incident: it must have happened several times. I see myself as a youngster, six or eight years old, seated on a summer evening on the steps of my grandmother's summerhouse—the rather simple dwelling that Southern planters often occupied in summer as a protection against the miasmas of the swamps. Supper is done; the little boy is satisfied. Behind him on the piazza are seated his grandmother, his uncle, perhaps an aunt; their low tones melt into the country silence. Across the piazza falls a rectangle of yellow lamplight from the open hall door. Within that door, the little boy knows, is the cot where he may sleep when he wishes. But now, backed by all that peace, he sits on the steps staring into the darkening woods. The night is alive with the chirring of insects and tree frogs; the stars come out and hang in the boughs; the Milky Way soars overhead. And the little boy is aware of all this strangeness, yet without fear. He is at home in a strange world. The peace of the family—his Southern inheritance—envelopes him; and the night and the stars are simply a challenge and a lure, felt only slightly as yet but there, a curtain to be parted when he wishes to rise and do so, as friendly as the door he will shortly open to his bedroom and comfortable cot.

If that little boy, now grown—indeed, grown old —is still an adventurer, it is partly because within those quiet moments he absorbed a peace that still sends him forth to prove its existence in the world. And, though he may have been lucky, there are hundreds of thousands of other Southerners, white and black, lucky in the same way, and to a greater or less degree. For, by the grace of God, we have maintained more of this essential peace than has the rest of the country. We are not aware of this, perhaps, and we are almost certainly not aware of what a necessary and invaluable resource it is for the new problems that face us. We're all confused, defending what we call our way of life. Meanwhile, our real way of life—the values by which we live—needs no defense except some daily cherishing. "A little lifting up of the heart is sufficient," said Friar Laurence. A little recognition of what we are, of the values we have and the desperate need, not only of the South but of the world, for these values, will take us safely—as safely as anyone may go through a dangerous world—into tomorrow, and the next day, and the future.

We are, all of us, the children of Adam and Eve, who, expelled from the Garden, saw, so Milton says,

"The world . . . all before them, where to choose Their place of rest and Providence their guide." But, more than this, we are the children of the South, who today, by the grace of God, stand upon the threshold of the world.

CHAPTER XV

Jeffersonian Tradition

THOSE WHO DOUBT the existence of a democratic tradition in the South should remember that the South produced Jefferson. Yet there are grounds for doubt, chief among them slavery and segregation. The treatment of the Negro is the Achilles' heel of Southern democracy, as Jefferson himself recognized. But among the whites from the beginning and increasingly now between whites and Negroes democracy exists, and presents an increasing challenge to segregation. Holding on to segregation, we struggle against this positive spirit within us, against ourselves. The decision to defend segregation is, therefore, a harsh, expensive one, not to be made unless absolutely necessary.

The white people of the South, among themselves, are probably the most democratic of all Americans. The British scientist Sir Charles Lyell, traveling in America in 1841–2, noted that Negro passengers on a river steamboat ate after the whites. "To a European," he wrote, "this exclusiveness seems the more unnatural and offensive in the southern states, because they make louder professions even than the northerners of democratic principles and love of equality. I must do them the justice, however, to admit that they are willing to carry out their principles to great lengths when the white race alone is concerned."

It is significant that Sir Charles noted this on a river steamboat, for the frontier was one of the main causes of American democracy, and the long-continued and renewed Southern frontier was one of the main causes of Southern democracy. On the frontier the situation is fluid. Men are on the make. Though they may have unequal resources, the chances for change are great. The man with an ax today may have lands tomorrow, and the man with lands, overreaching himself, may have to take up the ax again. Life has not yet settled into patterns; there are no classes, only individuals, competing or helpful, as the moment may suggest.

To some degree this economic fluidity has marked the entire history of the South. The lure of great and rapid gains—fortune through a single crop of cotton—made gamblers of most of us; and where there are gamblers, there are winners and losers. This economic uncertainty fostered the sense of democracy, of a fellow feeling among the whites. We were in the game together.

Again, the South has always been—and continues to be, though decreasingly—a rural area. People were scattered over the countryside, rich and poor at random. They met casually on the roads, or in the streets and on court-days, and at church on Sundays. Most of them were farmers; all of them were so close to the soil and so dependent upon it that they talked easily when they met of weather and crops and the market. There were no sharply defined classes, as in large cities, and few clearly outlined residential areas of rich or of poor.

This idea of the frontier and the farm as the home of democracy runs counter to the usual idea that the city, especially the industrial city, is that home. Both the frontier and the industrial city, being economically and therefore socially fluid situations, foster democracy. The settled farm, the ordered countryside tend to support a static economic and social order. But in the South, in antebellum days, even the plantations felt the pull of the frontier; and in postbellum days the frontier returned to the plantations themselves.

However, the democracy fostered by the industrial city isn't the same as that fostered by the frontier-touched farm. The former is primarily political: workers pressed together as a class use the power thus created to gain certain rights. The latter is, I think, more basic and human. A man on a frontier-touched farm is valuable, not because he can combine with a thousand others and assert jointly his power, but because the situation gives him considerable power as an individual and demands that he use it. Assured of such power, he is ready to share it with his neighbors, and to grant to his leaders large political powers. In the Old South it was these men who permitted the aristocrats to lead. "In the 1790's," says Francis Simkins, "there already existed in Tennessee the same regard for social superiors long characteristic of tidewater society." We have become so used in recent years to the cities serving as the spearhead of democracy that we forget that the city masses in so doing are often winning only the shadow of what the frontier farmers once possessed.

The democratic, leveling effect of frontier and farm was increased by our first two great wars. The Revolution was in part the expression of the rights of man. Clement Eaton gives an illustration from Anburey's *Travels* (1789) of these rights in action in Virginia. Anburey saw three countrymen enter Colonel Randolph's mansion and "sit down with the Colonel, pulling off their muddy boots and spitting on the floor, as they discussed the terms for grinding their grain at the Colonel's mill." It would appear either that Tennessee was more polite in 1790 than Virginia was in 1789, or, what is more likely, that the common man across the South accepted the leadership of the aristocrat without bowing before him.

The Civil War, with its hardships and its final defeat, deepened the sense of a common life among the whites. If the less privileged had ever doubted the leadership of the great—and to a degree they had—now, following them in battle, they doubted no longer. Leaders and common soldiers still treated one another in a casual, democratic, unmilitary fashion—sometimes, indeed, to their military misfortune, even perhaps to their final defeat. But men do not fight wars, they fight battles; the smoke and shock of the day is enough for the mind to hold; and amid that thunder the Southern leaders sat their horses easily, as though lounging on the piazzas back home. Under such personal leadership, men laughed, and fought, and lost the war, and came home. Though bitter over that loss, they had been through hell together, and were destined to become in time a band of brothers who would make of these battles one of the great epics of the western world: "Shiloh," "Gettysburg," "The Wilderness," they would say to one another, "and we were there."

If the frontier touched with democracy the whole South up to the Civil War, it almost overwhelmed it in the generation that followed. And now, and very consciously this time, the whites began to develop a white democracy as a protection against the Negroes. It had always been somewhat like this, though probably most of them weren't clearly aware of it. In antebellum days the whites of the South formed a democratic aristocracy based upon slave labor. Said Sir Charles Lyell: "The social equality which prevails here arises not so much from the spirit of a republican government, as from the fact of the whites constituting an aristocracy, for whom the Negroes work." Four fifths of the whites weren't aristocrats even in name. The other fifth, the slaveowners, were, however casually, also democratic because their position could be maintained only by the consent of the non-slaveowners. After the war, when the problem became one of maintaining white supremacy within a nation increasingly democratic in both theory and practice, white democracy became more of a reality than ever.

But while white democracy was becoming stronger, democracy itself, in part responding to the pressures of industrialization, was becoming stronger too, and the limited white democracy began here and there to waver. The Populist Movement, which stirred the nation in the nineties, was strongest in the South, where it was a rebellion within the white democracy. The most significant aspect of this rebellion was its tentative and brief extension of democracy to the Negro against whom white democracy existed. We have seen how Tom Watson urged white and Negro farmers to unite against the

Southern leaders, some of them the old plantation-owners, now become merchant-landlords, businessmen, and bankers, and most of them concerned mainly with railroad stocks, mills, and mining operations. These leaders went him one better: in spite of the long history of white brotherhood and the reported bitterness of Reconstruction, they voted Negroes in blocks and partly by this means licked the Populists.

But though this rebellion within the white democracy failed, it forced upon that democracy certain reforms. It also indicated a budding belief in the mind of the white Southerner that economic realities might take precedence over racial realities—that is, that white democracy might become democracy. For the time that notion was repressed. But now, fifty years of world revolution having transpired, it returns, this time in alignment with other forces, and moves toward a successful issue. What are those forces?

The first is the American democratic spirit, which, though limited at times, has always existed in the South. From 1787 to 1861 the South was not only a part of the nation but in many respects the leading part and proud of that leadership. The nation itself, a representative republic, in spirit a democracy, was continually growing more democratic, and, within racial limits, the South was growing more democratic with it. The strongest single force in this movement, Andrew Jackson, was himself a Southerner. The movement continued in the South after the Civil War, and from 1933 to the present, under the Roosevelt reforms, has affected the South as much as any part of the nation. For these reforms were for the benefit of the common man, white or black. Though it is true that in many things the Negroes did not receive their fair share, they did receive a share; and in farm elections, on economic issues, they vote alongside the whites without question.

According to the Southerner Gardner Murphy, writing even as far back as 1909, an inclusive democratic spirit has never been absent from the South: "We know, or ought to know, that that which really thrusts the negro (or any other weaker factor in our American environment) up into the consciousness of the majority is something deeper and more inexorable than any external power,—it is the hidden and intimate hand of our society itself; that silent, unyielding force of civil equalization to which we have committed, and have everywhere desired to commit, the keeping of our ultimate ideals and of our fundamental institutions."

This growing sense of democracy within the entire nation is closely connected with the part we have played in three world conflicts. American democracy has now become world democracy. We have long since passed the place where we could accept it simply as our own, with perhaps one ray of light directed from the Statue of Liberty toward the oppressed millions of Europe, and are forced to see ourselves as the leader of the democratic millions of the world.

The leader also, we hope, of the as yet uncommitted millions who, without knowing where they are going, are on the march. Communism, having already drawn millions to itself, presents to democracy such a challenge as it hasn't known before. If the tide of democracy had not been rising without this challenge, the challenge alone would have raised it.

We in the South today, therefore, face a double challenge: to further the cause of democracy throughout the world and to further it here at home. A double? Indeed, a triple: to wage this dual fight peacefully, for only thus can it be won. Omitting incidental conflicts, a modern war for democracy would be in its event a war, if not for annihilation, then for communism or whatever worse enemy the frustrated spirit of man might devise.

If more than this is needed to ensure our facing democratically our undemocratic race relations, we may remind ourselves that it is no new thing for the South to be concerned with the affairs of the world. We are indeed that part of the nation which most of the time has been most concerned with such affairs. If therefore today we consider our race problem in the light of world problems, it is the kind of thing we have usually done. Indeed, it is fair to say that the South has often been more concerned with the world beyond the Atlantic than with that beyond the Potomac. We have been historically a free-trade area; our economy was linked with the economies of the world. Today we live in a world increasingly international; cotton still binds together the mills of Japan and of South Carolina. The state of Georgia has not been noted for liberal advances in the field of race relations, yet former Senator George of that state, as chairman of the Senate Foreign Relations Committee, was pre-eminent for the good judgment with which he helped to pilot the nation through troubled international waters. The history of the last fifteen years shows that the South has taken a leading part, through its advocacy of the Atlantic

Charter, Lend-Lease, the Marshall Plan, and the United Nations, in shaping the course of our nation in the world.

Why should we chuck all this international experience and knowledge and try to settle our racial problem as if we were alone? We are sensitive to outside interference: we do hate to admit that our course of action is influenced by anybody at all. But our experience may make us especially effective in the world today. For the United States, as the leader of the democratic nations, faces the continual problem of persuading other people to change, and the continual danger of being charged by those people with the desire of ruthlessly interfering in their affairs. The South, having had its affairs interfered with, is sensitive in this matter; and Southern leaders are peculiarly fitted to soothe such irritations in the minds of others.

Considering, then, this preparation of the South for leadership in world affairs, and remembering that Southerners have been chief among those who in recent years have trimmed the sails of the nation to the winds of the world, we may have faith that, as we realize how important our handling of the racial problem is for the destiny of the nation, we shall carry such sail even here as the winds of the world will warrant.

We don't have to admit we're doing this; but that's all right. We Southerners are very dependent upon language, and oftentimes, after having used the accepted words, we face fairly realistically the situation.

Invisible Sun

To SAY THAT WE of the South believe in justice is only to say that we are human: most men believe in justice. But what is the nature of the justice we believe in? To what degree does it express the spirit of democracy which is growing stronger among us? To what degree the spirit of a lost or vanishing South?

Emil Brunner calls justice the law of institutions. The Greeks, whose views helped to form Christianity, said that justice is what belongs to a man. Paul Tillich speaks of it as love in action. There is another view that justice is redemptive: that which is needed for salvation.

As Brunner calls love the law of persons and as persons are involved in institutions, love is either mentioned or suggested in three of the above four descriptions of justice. How closely love and justice are related will become clear as we consider the racial situation in the South. It is enough to say here that love implies a personal relation, justice an abstract one; and the South hasn't had too much dealing with abstractions.

To the direct question "How does the white South feel about the justice of segregation?" there are many

answers. Some people will say without hesitation that
in the cold light of justice segregation is wrong. Some
are not sure. Some feel that, though it may be unjust,
it is necessary, or expedient. All thoughtful people will
admit, I think, that the system, at least in some details,
subjects the Negro to humiliations it is difficult to
justify in the light of the Judaeo-Christian tradition.
How have we justified our treatment of the Negro under slavery and segregation?

The first thing to realize is that we have tried to
justify it. This is itself a tribute to the Christian tradition. The Greeks and Romans didn't justify slavery;
they didn't have to. We have had to because we are
Christians, actually or nominally. Two things, however,
indicate that we have usually been afraid of our own
justifications. First, we have never tried to justify our
race relations in the full light of the Christian scriptures:
the light, that is, which shone in the face of Jesus, and
which not only flooded with splendor his own life but
also poured backward across the pages of the Old Testament and forward toward a coming Kingdom of God.
We have tried to justify them only by glancing passages
from the Bible, as, for instance, Noah's curse upon
Ham, and other references as vague as the fabulous
land of Nod. A second indication of our lack of belief
in our justifications is our tendency to grow shrill in
their presentation. We did that before the Civil War,
when we felt the forces of the North and the moral
forces of the world marshaling against slavery. We are
doing it now, when some of the same forces are mar-
shaled against segregation. These emotional outcries are
a sign of skepticism, not faith. Like the lady, we protest

too much. They are proof of the fact, however, that we have a religious tradition which represents man as a moral being living in a moral universe, and we have to believe, therefore, that what we do is morally justifiable.

In our differential treatment of the Negro, we have assumed that Negroes and whites are radically unlike, and that therefore what is just for one may be unjust for the other; that is, that there are two kinds of justice. Though the position of the Negro in respect to our courts is improving all the time, we still have occasion to admit, cynically or regretfully, that there is often a white man's justice and a Negro's justice. The fact that we are cynical or regretful suggests that there is somewhere in our minds an ideal of non-racial justice. Our failure generally to exemplify this ideal in law touches us a little more quickly than our failure to exemplify moral justice: the legal standard is more definite and more easily applicable. But whether it is a question of moral or of legal justice, we have defended "racial" justice on the ground of the supposed inequality of the races.

In general, however, and over the years, the white South has not justified its race relations, either by subjecting them to philosophic and religious scrutiny or by bringing them under the rule of law. If we ask why, we shall discover just where we stand today, and why we stand there.

The white South has not done this both because of the nature of the South and because of the fact of slavery and its continuing consequences after Emancipation. These two things are closely related: slavery was the most important factor in the creation of the South.

In the semi-feudal society of the Old South, relations tended to be personal and customary, not abstract and legal. This was true both of the relationships of the whites among themselves, and of the relationships of the whites with the Negroes. The sense of strong personal relations and obligations, related to the Southern family and clan, is illustrated by the "personal" politicians the South has always followed. The code of honor of the South was part of the same picture. Every man defended his own person and honor; he was both judge and executioner. Hodding Carter tells how this personal, extra-legal code operated in his own case in Greenville, Mississippi, as late as the 1930's. Even among the whites, therefore, abstract law has never been as important as it is in a typical modern democracy.

When we come to the relation between whites and Negroes, the importance of abstract law falls far into the background. The relationship was highly fuedal, and was that of the lord and his vassals or the patriarch and his family. Kindly slaveowners often spoke of their slaves as their children (sometimes they were, but this wasn't usually spoken of); they customarily spoke of them as "our people." In such a society, love and justice, the family and politics, were inextricably mixed. Good masters tried to be just, but the justice was personal, not according to any strict and written code (though, indeed, there was an unwritten code, the violation of which could bring social ostracism). Life for the slaves was a highly arbitrary and personal affair.

Now, the South continually made laws about slavery, but it generally admitted that the slaveowners were the law. In times of insurrection, or fear of insurrection, the entire white community became the law; at night, on the roads, the white patrol was the law; but generally the law was the slaveowner, and he guarded jealously his privilege and responsibility.

Emancipation brought a radical change, not so much in extending the law to cover the freedmen, as in making every white man a judge and policeman in regard to every Negro. It is true the Negro had been included under the Thirteenth, Fourteenth, and Fifteenth Amendments, but, except for the Thirteenth, these soon became dead letters. The only laws that were strictly enforced were those whose intent was to throw around the Negro a fence similar to slavery—that is, the segregation and disfranchisement laws. The white South is not averse to subjecting the Negro to law; it only objects to including him under a common law. Ordinarily, however, it relies not upon law but upon custom, enforced when necessary by every white man, whose general duty it is to see that every Negro stays in his place. This duty is not taught officially; you just pick it up from the atmosphere.

During Reconstruction it may have been taught officially. According to a Louisiana parish order of 1865, "It shall be the duty of every citizen to act as a police officer for the detection of offenses and the apprehension of offenders."

This is called "taking care" of the Negro, and ranges all the way from the truly kindly actions of the responsible landlord toward a tenant in need to the blustering announcement of some underprivileged white that he'll "take care of" some "nigger" who has overstepped bounds.

As wide as this range of care is, and as far as the good landlord is from the irresponsible white, they have been historically bound together. Says Major John De-Forest, one of the few clear-sighted Northerners who came South after the Civil War: "The 'high-toned gentleman' settled quarrels with persons of his own caste by his own hand; but, if he wanted a 'free nigger' run off or a Yankee 'emissary' mobbed, he winked to his humble and ferocious adherent [the poor white]. . . . In return he put up with Bill's petty pilferings, mendacities, and illicit dickerings with Negroes."

In the light of this background, we can understand the shock with which the white South received the Supreme Court decision of May 1954. Here, for the first time since the Fourteenth and Fifteenth Amendments had been pretty well invalidated by late-nineteenth-century Supreme Court decisions, the Constitution had been specifically interpreted to cover alike Negroes and whites. In arguing against this decision, the white South has said that you can't change custom by law. (The truth is that in a folk society you usually don't, but the loss of the Civil War and the writing of the post-war amendments headed us straight for an industrial society.) The South doesn't really believe this claim, for it changed some customs when it instituted segregation; and in the Prohibition fight, which the South led, it tried desperately to change custom by law. Nor can it be said that the Prohibition fiasco taught the South the lesson it claims to read in the 1954 decision; the Prohibition forces are stronger right now in the South than in any other part of the nation. Furthermore, in the crop-control laws the South ac-

cepts daily the breaking down of folkways by state-
ways, and finds itself bound to the state by all sorts of
benefits and penalties which would have been utterly
unacceptable two generations ago. This means that we
are moving from a folk to an industrial society, but
are trying to keep race relations on the customary—
that is, the folk—level.

In this emphasis upon concrete, personal relations
lie both the strength and the weakness of the South.
It is the principal strength that we carry into the industrial age. It is also our chief weakness, a minor detail of which is that we, like Robert Frost's little bird,
take everything said as personal to ourselves. More important is the fact that this emphasis upon the personal
is accompanied by a lack of respect for justice and the
law. We tend to substitute personal relations for law.
The worst side of this is that in regard to the Negro
every white tends to assume the prerogatives of the law;
the best side, which isn't good, is that even when the
white "loves" the Negro he does so without regard for
justice. The worst side needs no comment. It is the
best side, our paternalistic love for the Negro, which
really confuses both ourselves and him.

Ideally, and in its place, the paternal attitude is
creative. This is the father's attitude toward his child.
But the father expects the child to grow up and face
him like a man. The Southern whites could not expect
this of the Negroes; the system forbade it; in fact, toward the end of slavery the system even forbade teaching the slaves to read. Though the personal relations
of paternalism tended to break down under segregation,
in so far as they continued they were still touched with

this essential falseness: segregation was set up for keeps; the Negro was to remain, in relation to the white, a perpetual child.

Yet this essential falseness was touched with goodness. Years after the death of that uncle for whom ideals were a sin, I heard "Aunt Caroline" say—and the title is paternalistic—"When I die, the first person I'm goin' to see is my Jesus, and then I'll see Marse Guy." I suppose I'm prejudiced, but I find it hard to hear the falseness of that.

The more truly paternal the system was, the more often and surely it revealed within the Negro sparks of spirit and intelligence which proved to the discerning white that the system was wrong. Yet the white couldn't really question it. He loved the Negro, he said, but in his place; that is, in the system.

Another weakness of this paternalistic, personal attitude is that it puts too great an emphasis upon agreement, upon a surface peace. Justice was what the white man—under segregation, what any white man—said it was. There was no court of appeal. Therefore, Negroes, following the injunction of Jesus, agreed quickly with their white adversaries while they were in the way with them. This is a part of the general agreeableness of the South.

There is an interesting illustration of this in the *Journal* of Fanny Kemble. English herself, but married to a Georgia slaveowner, she once remonstrated with her husband for flogging a female slave. To her charge that the action was unjust, he replied that it was "disagreeable." It only ruffled the surface of his life; it stirred hers to the core. After the flogging, the slave doubtless became agreeable; peace was restored—the kind of peace, however, which Patrick Henry scorned.

There has recently been a wide outcry among Southern whites about the loss of peace and understanding between themselves and the Negroes. The Negroes aren't crying; they don't feel too keenly the ending of a peace that had been forced upon them. And it is being ended mainly because the Negroes don't care any longer to be loved by the whites. This naturally makes the whites angry, and they organize citizens' councils to make the Negroes let them love them again. For this privilege the whites will even use pressure and perhaps violence. They will have peace if they have to fight for it. This is typically Southern. This is where you come out if you try to substitute love for justice. This is loving a man to death.

The kiss of death, however, isn't simply the gift of the recently organized citizens' councils. It has been, throughout, the gift of slavery and of segregation. It was spiritual death in that it kept human beings in a childlike state; it became at times physical death, inflicted not only by the white upon the Negro but also by the Negro upon some whites and upon many Negroes. For what is the cause of the undue violence among Negroes—the even more than Southern violence among Negroes? I know the stock answer: *They are like that. They enjoy carving one another up. We just have to put up with it, and not punish them too severely, so long as they don't start carving up the whites.*

Neither carefully interpreted statistics nor common sense supports this explanation. The following is nearer the truth. Negroes are repressed both by the crowded and sordid conditions amid which many of them live and by the continual restraints of segregation. Angry against their neighbors because of the general restrictions, and angry against the whites because of the racial restrictions; unable to express this combined anger against the whites except under the probability of sudden and severe punishment, but able to express it against the Negroes under the probability of slight punishment or none at all, they grow violent among themselves. In addition, refused any large measure of responsibility by the whites, these "impulsive children" of ours remain irresponsible and flash their knives at a moment's notice.

There's more to it than this. They see that the white man can get them jailed on the slightest charge and, if he needs their services, can get them freed from the most serious. Therefore, they tend to disregard the law and do what they can to stay on the right side of the unpredictable white man. In place of law, they rely, like the true Southerners they are, upon personal favor, upon privilege—private law. In place of justice, they rely upon "love." But it's expensive, first for them, then for all of us: we love them to death. I am not surprised that they are growing suspicious of this tender attitude of ours.

Recently, in a Southern student conference, a white high-school student defended segregation because "it gives us a chance to be kind to Negroes." This goes Christianity one better by ensuring the presence of the poor, whose acceptance of our kindness paves our way to heaven. This student would have been interested to learn that a hundred years ago a slaveowner commended slavery to Frederick Olmsted in similar terms as "cultivating those habits of charitable feeling which the presence of the weak, the poor, and the dependent is always suggesting. . . ."

This basic unbalance between love and justice results in sentimentality—that is, unjustified emotion. It has been with us a pleasant task to deceive, if possible, the Negro, but more importantly ourselves; to hide from ourselves the fact that we were denying to the Negro the basic, general obligation of justice, while proffering him the personal gift of love. It is insulting to offer gifts while refusing obligations. Love can never be offered in place of justice; it may be offered in addition to justice.

It is not surprising to find that the South, being led toward sentimentality by its basic race and productive relations, fell into sentimentality in many other relations. In art, for instance. And, then, there's always Southern Womanhood, capitalized, and seated like patience on a monument upon its alabaster base!

These are the main reasons why the ideal of justice, although basic in the Judaeo-Christian tradition, has played such a relatively small part in interracial relations in the South. But, now, what of the future? Will the spirit of justice grow stronger within us? And, if it does, will it offer to segregation a growing challenge?

If we are moving—as we certainly are—from a more personal to a less personal society, if we are moving into a world increasingly institutionalized, we are also moving into a world where justice and the law must receive greater emphasis. If it is an increasingly democratic world—as it seems to be—then justice will become increasingly democratic.

But there are more particular reasons than this why in the South today there is a growing desire for a common justice for all men, white and black. First of all, the whites grew tired of policing the Negroes and enforcing a Negro justice. I grant there are many men, underprivileged in one way or another, who enjoy the authority that custom has given the white over the Negro. Seventy-five years ago, when the whites of the South has just concluded that this policing job was necessary, I dare say most of them accepted it as part of their responsibility. Edgar Gardner Murphy suggests, however, that as early as 1910 the policing had begun to grow burdensome. He reports an older friend as saying: "I sometimes feel that I have ceased to be the citizen of my country, and have become, instead, but the citizen of a race."

Since then, five decades have passed—two generations—and times have become tremendously better. Today many a Southern white will be moved to abandon segregation more from a desire to get out from under the burden of maintaining it than from the obligation to do justice—especially when the burden grows more oppressive with national, indeed world, opposition, and more complex with changing customs. We mingle with Negroes at games on government reservations because enforcement there is taken out of our hands: we are on federal property, we have no responsibility. Take Shaw Air Force Base, near Sumter, South Carolina, where at integrated athletic contests white citizens' council leaders may be seen sitting by Negroes and chatting with them. But when they come away from the Base and back downtown they assume again, with sober faces, the policeman's role. A part of the South's present excitement over maintaining segregation is due to the fact that it senses how little it really cares, and is trying to whip up enthusiasm for an attitude no longer deeply believed in.

But in addition to this growing desire to slough off an unwanted responsibility, there is, as the second ground for increasing interracial justice, a growing sense of responsibility to all the members of our society. Call it the humanitarian spirit of our time. We live in a nation that is increasingly concerned about religion; and as this religion is Christianity, with its prophetic tradition of social justice, we become increasingly, though more slowly, concerned about justice. We live in a nation that is democratic in spirit, and therefore humanitarian, and therefore concerned about justice. Even Billy Graham, Southern-born leader of the Protestant masses, now turns his guns against segregation.

In the third place, the Negro himself is touched by this spirit. He begins to demand justice, plain justice, the justice accorded by equals to equals. This demand is amplified by the growing demand of the colored peoples of the world, and by the growing power of the Negro in our country. With his economic advance, especially since the opening of World War II, has gone a political advance. In certain Northern cities and states he holds the balance of power. He also gains power in national politics because of the importance to the nation of the good will of the colored races everywhere.

These demands for justice reinforce our humanitarian desire. For justice is a two-way street. It isn't simply granted by the group in power out of simple goodness. True, the goodness is there, the desire to be just. But, for most people, this desire expresses itself only as there is a demand for it, and defines itself according to that demand. Speaking of slavery, Fanny Kemble says: "How very torpid the sense of justice is apt to lie in the breasts of those who have it not awakened by the preëmptory demands of others." Today powerful forces in the world are demanding justice for colored people, and—partly for selfish, partly for unselfish reasons—our hearts are seconding the demand. There are, indeed, tides in the affairs of men; and good deeds impossible in one age become commonplaces in another.

Turning toward justice, therefore, we realize even as we turn that, in spite of our irritation and displeasure at the demands urged upon us by the Negroes, this is what we want to do. We find here the satisfaction of dealing with a worthy opponent. We love children; they give to a perpetually aging world a perennial freshness. But to treat men and women as if they were children is a dangerous sham, and in the bottom of our hearts we know it. Faced with the rugged hardships of life, as in crises we always are, we need about us men, agreeing or disagreeing, but men. It is the common manhood within us, not the privileges we hold, which hardens us to endure the trials of life. And manhood in us is increased by the manhood in others. Every Negro, therefore, who stands up as a man, though he stand up to us, is a gift to our manhood; and though for a little

while we try to stare him down and force him down,
we know in the bottoms of our hearts that his cool,
appraising gaze is what we need. Slowly we find our
condescending good will turning to respect, and in this
mutual respect we shall hammer out justice together. In
such moments of recognition we realize that we live
by an invisible sun within us, and that one of its names
is justice.

The fourth ground for believing in the coming extension of interracial justice in the South is, perhaps,
only a result of the third. It is the tendency in critical
moments to examine the bases of our life. As we are
social beings, to examine these bases is to examine society, and to examine society is to raise the question of
justice.

We have assumed we have been just to the Negro;
indeed, we have hardly let ourselves raise the question.
Circumstances now are raising it for us. There is no
doubt that we want to be just; most men do, only they
differ as to what justice is. Now, concern about justice
and the passion for justice are created in most men by
the experience of injustice. As we suffer injustice, we
desire justice, first for ourselves and then, somewhat
incidentally and partly as a result of the overflow of
life within us, for others. Our Southern way of life is
breaking down; many of us are inclined to feel that
this is the result of some injustice done us. We are
therefore asking ourselves the questions: What is justice? What is interracial justice?

Let us take justice at its simplest, in the family.
Though by no means always attained even here, it is
theoretically simple here because of the basic equality

of the members. The wider the group included in our thought, the more difficult it is to realize this basic equality and to imagine laws and customs applicable to all. Tocqueville remarked that "men are much more forcibly struck by those inequalities which exist within the same class than by those which may be noted between different classes." The whites of the South have accepted the ideal of a basic equality among themselves; it remains for us to accept it as between whites and Negroes.

This is no more than the Christian ideal we profess: sons of God and therefore brothers. The words are easy to repeat but hard to realize. Yet they can be realized by those who have the courage. If we turn upon man, ourselves included, Ortega's "tragic, ruthless glance," we shall see him for the lonely creature he is, a pilgrim on the earth, stumbling out of a night too dark to remember and moving how quickly he does not know into another night too dark to imagine. In such a view there is no room for white justice and black justice. Encircled as we are by infinite darkness, skin color does not matter.

If we in the South desire to be more faithful to the Judaeo-Christian ideal of justice—and both the times and our hearts demand this—let us ask ourselves what life is; and, having realized in the search the great oneness of mankind, we shall begin to reshape our institutions so that justice shall become stronger and love purer.

For these several reasons, and perhaps for others, the desire for justice among both Negroes and whites is growing stronger in the South. Call it humanitarianism;

call it the social gospel. The fact remains that we are
more concerned than our fathers were how to live together in the world. It may be because it is becoming
more difficult to live together in the world; it may be
that our conscience is the reflection of world movements. No matter. The sun of justice shines more
brightly within us, and the shadows of injustice fall
more darkly across our path. Perhaps we have built, all
unintentionally, a world which demands that we follow
more closely the Judaeo-Christian tradition. Fortunately,
that tradition still exists in our hearts and demands for
itself a sterner allegiance.

It may express itself even in the faint pang of
conscience which Katherine Lumpkin (of *The Making
of a Southerner*) felt as a little girl when in crowded
streetcars, knowing it was her right to be seated though
a Negro be made to stand, she preferred to remain
standing "rather than have a fleeting glimpse of the still,
dark faces in the rear of the car, which seemed to stare
so expressionlessly into space."

It may be something still fainter. A group of white
women in a neighboring community were recently
planning a program for the World Day of Prayer.
Though nobody would say so, apparently the difficulty
was whether the Negro women of the community
should be included. Finally one woman, more realistic
than the rest, said: "Look here. We're all grown-up. If
we wish to invite the Negro women, let's do so; if we
don't, let's forget it." "Oh, but," one lady objected, "we
have to consider our consciences."

As, indeed, we do. The pale conscience of this pale
lady may never foment revolution, but it is one of the

factors in social change; and when hers becomes the common conscience deep within us, it isn't to be scorned. Working with world forces, it is undermining the wall of segregation, which, however useful it may have been, now has become an obstacle to free endeavor.

As we remove this wall, as we stand in a more just relation to one another, as we tend toward equality of opportunity, our manners will assume again something of the authority and the charm they had in the Old South. With this difference: they will now be the manners of equality. Having specialized so long in manners as opposed to skills; having been so long learning how to be agreeable; living still in an agreeable land and in a social order, for all its rough edges, agreeable too, we shall tend to discover the manners proper to the new relations. Courtesy, the flower of manners, prides itself upon the ability to do the proper thing. As actual relations change, the proper things to do change with them.

Finally, as we heal the basic rift in our society, we shall be able to disagree without becoming disagreeable and argue without becoming violent. No longer, then, will our manners be the down upon the wormy peach, but the heart's unfeigned expression.

CHAPTER XVII

Central Fire

WE COME AT LAST to the central fire burning at the heart of the South, which, fanned into a blaze by the winds of our time, will do more than anything else to destroy segregation. This is the Christian spirit of love.

To this point we had to come. If, as John said and Jesus showed and we believe, God is love, love is both the beginning and the end of our endeavors, the source and the goal of our thinking. Even while discussing justice, a concern of this world, we suggested its kinship with love, which abides beyond space and time. The same creative spirit is at work in democracy, in technology, and in the forward thrust of the pioneer. Approaching the end of our study, therefore, we consider this essential spirit, and ask to what degree it is ours.

I know how tricky love is, what false shapes it assumes. And the times are insisting that we question that paternalistic love which has tempered race relations in the South. But the insistence comes partly from within our hearts.

The growing importance of this spirit in the South

is indicated by the attitude of our religious leaders. Contrast the present situation with that of 1861. The South entered the Civil War with its religious leaders not only supporting slavery, but leading the fight to maintain slavery. Today a few ministers here and there frankly defend segregation; the vast majority are as yet saying nothing; the top-flight men, with very few exceptions, are opposed to segregation.

One of these, Dr. Edward S. Grant, of Louisiana, spoke as follows to the 1957 General Assembly of the Southern Presbyterian Church: "We face in the world today an outbreak of color conscience such as no other generation has ever seen. This is but the fruit of the teaching of the Christian church around the world, for it has developed in men's hearts everywhere the desire for personal freedom, and racial freedom."

This was not true in 1861. Some two years ago, at a Citizens' Council rally in South Carolina, the chairman introduced a ministerial advocate of segregation with the words: "When our boys went forth in '61, they were followed by the prayers of the preachers of the South. It is therefore appropriate that we open this meeting with an invocation by Rev. Blank." There should have been a realist there to awaken the dreamers. "Mr. Chairman," he would have cried, "if the massed clergy of the South couldn't do any better in '61 than they did, this poor chap might as well go home and crawl into bed."

This is sometimes admitted, even by the segregationists. In 1955, Robert B. Crawford, president of the Defenders of State Sovereignty and Individual Liberties, told a meeting of the Charlottesville, Virginia, chapter: "The worst obstacle we face in the fight to preserve segregated schools in the South is the white preacher. The patriots of Reconstruction had the preachers praying for them instead of working against them."

I do not maintain that our religious leaders are relatively as powerful as they were in '61; but I do maintain, first, that the church today is not the captive of the race issue that it was in '61. At that time the great majority of the Negroes were second-class members of the church; the church, therefore, was moved to defend the existing racial controls partly because they were also its own controls. At the present time the white church has no control over Negroes, and is therefore less concerned that the existing social controls be maintained. Certain members of the church, as citizens, may be as concerned as they were in '61, but leaders of the church find the matter less important. I maintain also that the South is still religious, and that therefore the attitude of her religious leaders today indicates what her own attitude will be tomorrow. And that will oppose segregation.

Indeed, the essential spirit of Protestantism, the predominant form of Christianity in the South, opposes segregation as it opposed slavery. It is true that antebellum Protestant leaders were able, by means of the doctrine of vocation, to warp the individualistic spirit of Protestantism to the support of a stratified, feudal society. But only as a *tour de force*. The stratified society of the South has never had a solid religious base, as did the feudalism of the Middle Ages, and has therefore always been in process of crumbling. The present crumbling of segregation is in part the continuation of this process.

But, deeper than Protestantism, the essential spirit of Christianity is opposed to segregation. What is this essential spirit? It is not justice and the law; Paul saw that. As fundamental as these are, there is something which was before the law, out of which the law grew, and which will continue after the law. This is the spirit of divine love, which, through justice, creates human institutions in which it may be at home.

In all ages Christians have realized this, and have connected this spirit with the person of Jesus. More than ever is this true today. The following incident illustrates both the tendency and its obstruction. Recently, on a Sunday morning, a Negro lieutenant from a near-by air base entered a white church in the Deep South and quietly took a seat near the back. A disturbed usher hurried to the minister and whispered: "What shall I tell him?" The minister, feeling it would be best for the usher to assume authority, replied: "Try to imagine what Jesus would say and tell him that." The happy suggestion fell upon stony ground. The usher whispered to the lieutenant: "You have a church of your own; you'd better go there." The lieutenant walked out, together with all the white soldiers from the base. Later, in a meeting of the church officers, the minister said: "I can't imagine Jesus turning anyone away from the door of his church." Apparently some of the officers could. Or perhaps they just couldn't imagine Jesus. However blind they may have been, they were at least being directed toward the light.

Christian theologians have not only recognized this light, this divine spirit of love, in the person of Jesus; they have also acknowledged him as the incarnation of the Universal Spirit, the eternal source of being, the beginning and the end. This is also the impression produced upon those whom we honor as saints.

It is an impression of marvelous grace and love. John, the Beloved Disciple, felt it so keenly that the love of Christ, and the love of God, and the necessary response of love on the part of man were always on his lips; and the fierce Saul of Tarsus, now Paul, sang in the thirteenth chapter of First Corinthians a noble hymn to love.

Not only did Jesus so reveal this spirit that men saw in him its perfect expression; he also, upon inquiry, spoke of it, and made love the first and the last commandment. Spoke, they said, with authority. In the twilight of his life, his disciple Philip, sensing the coming of the night and seeking something to cling to, begged that he would show them the Father. "Have I been with you so long, and yet you do not know me, Philip?" Jesus asked. "He who has seen me has seen the Father."

Those men, therefore, who possess the spirit of Jesus possess the spirit of love; and, possessing it, they know, as he has taught them, that this is the spirit of God.

It is the spirit that struggles to express itself in the lives of those who call themselves Christians. It is the flame they cherish and sometimes by God's grace see burst into a blaze. We ask, then, are segregation and racial discrimination fuel for this flame, good works done in the world which encourage and kindle the doubting heart? Or are these actions cold water quenching the inner fire? Whatever justification we may find for them, is it possible to justify them on the altar of this human-divine love, which burns, however flickeringly, within the heart? Are they such first fruits as can be offered to God?

In the light of all that has been said in earlier pages, I think we must answer no. Still, however, some of us may doubt. We see that most of the reasons offered for segregation are, upon careful examination, flimsy; we see that the dangers against which it is supposed to protect us are for the most part unreal; we see that some of our attitudes in the matter are simply habits, and others a cloak for selfishness, and still others the result of the confusion of life, which is sacred, with segregation, which is only one of its perishing forms; we see, finally, that these old habits stand in the way of certain positive forces within us struggling for expression, chief among them the spirit of love which Jesus expressed and commanded—and yet—and yet—we are afraid it can't be done. We think it ought to be; we really don't want to defend it ourselves; but we're afraid it can't be—at least not now.

Perhaps this vague fear exists in the minds of many Christians. If so, we should name it for what it is. For its proper name may shock us into a deeper awareness of ourselves, and in the fantastic world we have created in the South, that would be all to the good.

It is lack of faith. Faithlessness. No more and no less. If we had more faith in God, we should have less fear. If we were filled with faith, we should have none. (No man attains, except at moments, this peak. Yet it is the peak toward which we climb.)

As we believe in love—which is to say, as we

have love—we do not have fear. As we are afraid, then, we lack love, and lack faith in a God of love. Our fearfulness is the mark of our faithlessness, and simply means that the essential fire of Christianity burns but flickeringly upon the altar of our hearts.

How may that flame be steadied? By placing it alongside the original, the brightest of all its expressions, the life of Jesus. Contemplating that shining example, we shall find his spirit growing within us and the fears that now cling to our hearts like miasma along Southern ditches in summer dispersing before the beams of the rising sun.

What we need in the South today is men of large, generous, and magnanimous natures. Where shall we find them? Though one may not say where the spirit of God will move, it is possible we shall find them more frequently among Negroes than among whites. For we have had the things of the world; they have often had nothing but faith. I recall once, on a summer afternoon, sitting in the Negro church here at home. The congregation was singing some hymn and I was singing with them. I forget what it was, but it must have carried a deep assurance. For as I gazed through the open door across the summer fields beyond, I shouldn't have been surprised to see Jacob's ladder rising there in the corn, and the radiant angels ascending and descending upon it.

As we have faith, we shall develop the institutions of a more Christian society. It is not easy to give institutional shape to love; it means transforming it into justice. Regardless of this difficulty, the source of our strength—and of our weakness—is clear: out of the heart proceed the issues of life. As our hearts are sensitive both to God's presence and to human need, as we yield ourselves to his encompassing love, we shall act well, and shall build, in these changing times, a more Christian society.

One other word, farfetched though it may be. As has been evident throughout this book, I believe that we can change only as we have it in us to change. The actions of the contemporary world may release the motives; but these will be the motives that our characters and our training suggest; and our actions will be, largely, the children of our past. I do not deny the creative quality of men, nor our ability to make radical changes. In many cases, however, even such changes will, upon examination, show their roots in the past. Therefore, I am interested in the past: our roots sink into it; much of our life flows from it. We should starve without the enveloping air, which may stand for the future; we should starve as completely without the soil, which may stand for the past.

Now, when I read the New Testament, I notice a strange thing. The life of Jesus combines, in perhaps an unprecedented fashion, a sense of relaxation and a sense of urgency. He gives the impression of abundant time, and yet few men have walked a swifter path to death. Just three years. He chatted with his friends and considered the lilies of the field and sternly, against Peter's persuasion, went up to Jerusalem. He was never in a hurry, yet always on time. He kept his date with destiny in the small events of life and in the great.

It's the way a man would like to live. It's the way —it's the way the South perhaps has some training in, and therefore some hope of improvement in. We bring from the past the sense of relaxation. Perhaps we have overdone it. We have been too casual, too satisfied; we have been complacent. But today, as we have seen, we are moving into a world of widening horizons and a chillier atmosphere; a world of great challenges, racial and industrial, especially made for us; challenges which demand that we use as never before our simple neighborliness, our good nature—unfortunately often superficial—our relaxed attitude. In brief, challenges that seem designed, indeed fated, for us. If we thus perceive them, we shall know that we have come to the kingdom for such a time as this; and we shall begin to move forward with an easy stride, relaxed still but going somewhere now, walking as it were between the past and the future, holding the hand of each.

It's a good way to walk. It's the way Jesus walked, who came not to destroy but to fulfill. It's a way we have some talent for, perhaps, here in the South.

CHAPTER XVIII

Divided Heart

THE BOOK COULD END HERE. For we have analyzed the
race problem in the South and described the positive forces, within us and beyond us, which are
working toward a solution. I feel, however, that we
haven't yet said the main thing, haven't outlined the
over-all problem, haven't quite seen the forest for the
trees. We have examined race relations in detail. Can we
see them as a whole?

We think of the races as distinct. Distinct and in
some way opposed: whites *versus* Negroes. One of the
fears we considered, and dismissed as unfounded, was
that Negro culture, so-called, might overwhelm white
culture. We found that Negro culture differs from white
culture mainly in such ways, most of them minor, as
might be expected of the culture of an underprivileged
minority; and that even these differences are rapidly dis-
appearing as the Negro rises in economic and social
status.

But is there, possibly, a single Southern culture,
and what are the implications of this possibility?

Let us recall both our own childhood and the childhood of earlier generations of Southerners, white and colored. Historically, it has been one childhood, white and Negro children growing up together. This was most true under slavery, decreasingly true with the break-up of the master-slave relationship and the plantations and with the urbanization of the South. Yet even today many white and Negro children grow up together, friendly, relaxed, and for the first years unaware that either black or white means anything at all.

Except as all sensuous impressions mean much to children. The world is new to them. New, fresh, and inviting. Never again will early apples taste so sweet, nor men and women seem so strange and godlike. The impressions of these years sink deep into the heart, and, though they may be apparently erased by later events and ideas, or buried beneath the commonplaces of time, they are still alive, speaking to us in dreams, whispering in the quiet moments of the day. What these impressions generally tell us in the South is that people are people, white and colored together.

Unless our childhood has been very unhappy, we tend to remember with pleasure the events of those years. There is our lost Eden. Its bright impressions return from time to time to criticize our shopworn days. Sometimes, of course, when the problems of life become too hard and the responsibilities too heavy, men refuse to face them and drift on the ocean of the past. But those who do face them and tackle them creatively do so because of an ideal rooted in earlier days, perhaps even in childhood, when the world was fresh and young. They are those who, in Thoreau's words, have refused to "learn from experience" that life is bad and hopeless. The past, then, is both an asylum for the defeated and an arsenal for fighters.

Today, of course, we're terribly afraid of Freud: the past is only our mother's womb, and the longing to return there is, to say the least, indecent. But the past is also our father's house: the social structure of that early period when, even though human, we were apt to be happy. And, unless we flee from our responsibilities, or pass indifferently by them, we face them in the best, the most positive spirit we know; and that is, typically, the spirit of the child.

We go into the world to seek our father's house; the Prodigal Son is always headed home.

Or, passing beyond our individual memories of the undivided world of childhood, let us consider the group memory of the South, especially of the Civil War. The fact that we seldom recall the role of the Negro in that war does not mean that we have really forgotten it. We have not forgotten the war, and perhaps the most astounding fact about it was the loyalty of the slaves, which, said John T. Trowbridge, the Northern visitor, in 1865, "challenged the admiration of the world." Though this loyalty was not, as the vague tradition maintains, absolute, by and large the slaves did protect their masters' families and further their masters' interests, even though by so doing they may have damaged their own. Why did they do this? Partly because they were Southerners, helping to defend their native land, helping to defend, as they believed, their fields and firesides. They knew life as a fact, freedom hardly as a theory. It is significant that the Southern whites never expected the slaves to act otherwise, so confident were they of their loyalty.

Why doesn't this astounding fact bulk larger in the tradition of the Civil War? Probably because of the overwhelming tradition of Reconstruction. The white South still fears that ghost, the Negro of 1865–76. The division and conflict of those years has tended to blot out the earlier oneness. Yet I am sure that the battle light of the sixties, falling across the Southerner's heart, is still tinged, however faintly, with a warm sense of the oneness of the South, white and black, in that tragic time.

More significant than our individual memories or our traditions is our art. Our stories, of course, but most of all our songs. Whose are the songs of the South? Are they about Negroes or whites? The spirituals, of course, are about Negroes, and by Negroes; but the Negroes made them out of the revival songs of the whites. They are Southern art, therefore, born of our people, binding us together in the infinite longing they express. But what of the folk songs—even those made by Stephen Foster? "Dixie," "My Old Kentucky Home," "Carry Me Back to Old Virginia," "Darling Nellie Gray," and the rest? The images these songs contain and the emotions they express are those of a land that holds within its gracious hands both whites and Negroes, alike in their joys and sorrows, their failure and success.

I know it's claimed that these songs represent the dual South, of superior whites and inferior Negroes, and therefore inculcate this attitude in us who sing them. I cannot agree with this. They do come out of the dual South and picture it; but what they express, and mainly arouse in us, is the pathos and joy of the human situation, the binding reality that underlies even the Southern division of race.

Even if this be true, you object, these are only songs; this is only a dream. So, in the long run, is life. The songs a people sing, the dreams they dream are the people themselves.

But even more fundamental than our common songs and dreams is the fact that as Southerners we are inclined to dream, to lean away from the practical toward the artistic. The present looms large; the passing moment is filled with attraction. The white South may have learned this from the colored, as the South Carolinian Ravenel suggests in his *Journal*, at Christmas 1866, when he said the Negroes "are taking their time, easy and happy and thinking but little of the future. Perhaps there is true wisdom at least in this, viz. to enjoy the free bounties of God in moderation and with thankfulness, without that constant feverish struggle after the acquisition of *more*. The past has taught us lessons of this kind. The accumulations of years, the gatherings from much toil and saving, where are they?"

However the South came to this view, it is the view of a pious people, a people so entranced with the world as they receive it that they hesitate to change it into anything else; and we have the word of a Southern poet and scholar, John Crowe Ransom, that piety is in some degree an aesthetic attitude.

Watch a Southerner at work, and you may conclude that here you have found in action the ideal of that rebellious New Englander Thoreau: "Life is more to be enjoyed than used." Thoreau complained that most men repeated without understanding the Shorter Catechism definition of man's chief end as glorifying God and enjoying him forever. He should have come South. Here he would have found the enjoyment, though whether always of God one might doubt.

Yet, it is only fair to remember, even though we do not define religion, that the South is still the most religious section of the country. Certainly piety, that loving and, as Ransom suggests, disinterested attachment to present things, is strongest here. The Southerner leans away from the practice toward the poetry of life; and my guess is that he does this primarily because the longtime association of whites and Negroes in a certain economic situation has persuaded him that this is the best thing to do. About the most impractical thing you can do in the South is to insist upon being practical: the climate of opinion is against it.

As we search our memories, then, both individual and collective, and as we contemplate our dreams and ourselves the dreamers, we feel, I think, that we of the South are one. But what do we say? We say we are two; we say we are the white race and the colored race, divided by law and custom.

If in the deep heart's core we are one, it is disastrous to say we are two. For a lie about one's own nature is an ultimate lie. To lie about the world, or to be mistaken about it, is dangerous: the supposedly cold line may be hot. But to lie about oneself, or to be mistaken about oneself, especially in such a fundamental fashion as we have just suggested, is to set the heart against the brain in a civil war far more disabling than the last. I have felt for a long time that the heart of the white South was divided between the desire for justice and decency and the desire for continued privilege. Patrick Henry said long ago we knew we should free the slaves, but, alas, life was too pleasant. Such a division means the weakening of moral identity, the tendency of the one self to break in two. But our division may be far more critical than this. Properly fearful of abstractions, we here by a violent abstraction break the unity of our life apart. We draw a cold line down through our hearts and call it segregation. Life, which through our personal and social memories—and, indeed, through many continuing experiences—we know to be one, we call two. No wonder we are afraid of abstractions; we are dying of one.

I'm not talking about racial amalgamation; I don't see any use. That's a bridge we have crossed, and will cross when we wish, regardless of what we say. I'm not saying that anything should or should not be done. I'm simply saying that, apparently, a certain situation exists, and that the first step in wisdom is to recognize it. If the situation involves us as completely as I have suggested, to fail to recognize it is to lose, or perhaps never to gain, our moral identity. And that, perhaps, is what we have been doing in the South.

But we are Southern even in the way we do it; modern only in that the loss of moral identity is a characteristic of modern, exploitative man. Our way is forthright and simple. For the typical modern, however, loss of identity occurs in the complex, abstract, unimaginable productive order. The man who enters that dark forest does so largely because of the apparently clear and quick economic gain. The gain is clear and quick. The cost, however, is indirect, devious, and usually unrecognized. Modern man is like the chief character of Henry James's "Beast in the Jungle." That individual feared that at some unforeseen moment life would leap upon him like a jungle beast. But the years passed and nothing happened. Then, in the last moments of the story, the realization comes that pages and years ago it had happened: the beast had leaped and the man had been destroyed. So modern industrial man, threading the jungle of money and machines, blinded and dazed by both, turns a corner here, enters an alley there, follows a trail until it disappears, and he is left alone in the wood, surrounded by shadowy, lost people like himself but aware only of his uncertainty and the brush whipping his eyelids. He may not even know he is lost, but he wanders in circles just the same.

I'll say this for the South: there's no such subtlety about being lost down here. We have chosen a simple method, befitting our broad landscapes and expansive natures. We even talk of being lost; sin and salvation have never passed from our vocabulary. In the personal society of the South, in the personal heaven overarching it and in the sight of the personal God withdrawn somewhere within, sin is simple, concrete, and recognizable. We don't alienate ourselves through a thousand apparently inconsequential actions; ruthless and violent, we split our hearts in two.

The advantage of this is that we can see what we've done. The Negro is always with us, as we are with him. There he is before our eyes, the symbol of our sin, the living reminder to our hearts that our words are wrong. In contrast to the extended long-division through which your typical modern loses his moral identity, this is simple short-division: one divided by two equals one half. But when you begin to unwrap the emotions that, like miasma along Southern ditches, swathe our divided hearts, shielding them if possible from our unhappy eyes, you may conclude that, for complexity, modern industrial man is by contrast a piker. For with our deepest hearts we love our "sin," realizing that in those lost associations we found, if any-where in this divided world, salvation; but with our brains and the false standards of our maturity we hate ourselves for loving our "sin," and praise ourselves for maintaining a *separate but equal* "salvation." What our hearts call salvation, our brains call sin; and what our brains call salvation, our hearts call sin; and, regardless of what the truth is, there's little health left in us.

Except the fact that we can never quite forget that we are sick. We know we need a physician. Be-neath our thickest crust of complacency, our conscience continually stirs, disturbed, however faintly, by the presence of a dark, friendly people whom we insist upon calling foreign.

I wouldn't blur with these running comments what I consider the basic situation in the South: that through the processes of history and the grace of God we have been made one people, and that it is disastrous to talk and act as if we were two. If, on the contrary, we would play the game wholeheartedly together, if we would be our deepest selves, there is no telling what great age might develop in the South. For here we are, two originally dissimilar people fused by the fires of history, one already but lacking yet the courage to accept the fact. Are we, the white people of the South, going to admit that men of Anglo-Saxon blood have grown too old to learn? That the virtues and the faults which are typically ours are fixed forever? Here we are, as of today, with a hard drive that might well be softened by some compliance, a pride that might well be softened by humility, an economic interest that might well be softened by a sense of the living moment. Do I say such things might well be? It is more accurate to say they are. For these things have already happened in the South. The white Southerner is the man he is because he has lived among Negroes, and they are the people they are because they have lived with him. We don't have to do anything about it; we have only to accept the fact. The basic fact of our lives. The South has always preferred facts to theories. Here is the grand chance to prove that we are indeed Southerners.

The first requirement for the success of a man—or a society—is that he accept the existing situation and face the present. Bemused by a past both tragic and disastrous, the South has hardly done this. Beyond mere acceptance is love. "It is not enough," said Nietzsche, "to accept fate, you must love it." If Southerners could rise to the level of loving passionately, not only their hills and valleys, as they do, but also the rich and varied configuration of people, black and white, who dwell therein, with the untold possibilities for achievement which lie in such association, we should not only solve our greatest problem, one of the two major problems of the world today, but our age would become a challenge to generations as yet unborn, even as the singers of Elizabethan England still challenge the hearts and the voices of men.

It is always true, in a sense, as Shelley wrote of his own generation, that

> *The world's great age begins anew,*
> *The golden years return. . . .*

This may become true of the South today. Behind the problems that face us stand unimaginable opportunities, waiting to test our proverbial gallantry and courage. We have never been afraid of a fight; we hardly admit yet that we lost the Civil War. Let us accept now such a challenge as will astonish the world.

ACKNOWLEDGMENTS AND NOTES

I AM GRATEFUL to the Fund for the Republic both for the grant-in-aid that made this book possible and for the confidence shown in leaving entirely to me the conception and the execution of the work. The opinions expressed are my own; indeed, the Fund for the Republic will never know what they are unless it reads these pages.

I should also like to express my thanks to the authors and publishers of those books, listed below, from which I have quoted directly.

Page 11 Howard Odum: *The Way of the South* (New York, 1947), p. 116.
Page 28 Mary Boykin Chesnut: *A Diary from Dixie* (New York, 1905), p. 321.
Page 50 *News and Courier* (Charleston, S.C.), January 25, 1898. In George B. Tindall: *South Carolina Negroes, 1877–1900* (Columbia, S.C., 1952), p. 300.
Page 54 W. P. Livingstone: *The Race Conflict* (London, 1911), p. 185.
Page 80 Hylan Lewis: *Blackways of Kent* (Chapel Hill, 1955), p. 234.
Page 85 Hobart M. Corning, report of, in *Race Relations Law Reporter*, February 1957 (Vol. II, no. 1), p. 212.
Page 87 Vernon L. Wharton: *The Negro in Mississippi, 1865–1890* (Chapel Hill, 1947), p. 227.
Page 88 D. R. Hundley: *Social Relations in Our Southern States* (Philadelphia, 1860), p. 219.
         Wharton: op. cit., pp. 228–9.
Page 98 Quoted by W. P. Livingstone: *The Race Conflict* (London, 1911), pp. 168–9.
Page 104 Quoted by Henry T. Thompson: *Ousting the Carpetbagger from South Carolina* (Columbia, S.C., 1927), p. 30.
Page 107 F. B. Simkins and R. H. Woody: *South Carolina During Reconstruction* (Chapel Hill, 1932), p. 462.
         In Tindall: op. cit., p. 24.

Page 108 In Katherine Lumpkin: *The South in Progress* (New York, 1940), p. 205.
Tindall: op. cit., p. 258.
E. Franklin Frazier: *The Negro in the United States* (New York, 1949), p. 146.
Francis B. Simkins: *A History of the South* (New York, 1953), pp. 507–8.

Page 109 Quoted in John Temple Graves: *The Fighting South* (New York, 1943), p. 136.
Simkins: op. cit., p. 595.
William A. Percy: *Lanterns on the Levee* (New York, 1941), p. 270.

Page 110 Reported in *Southern School News*, Jan. 6, 1955 (Vol. I, no. 5), p. 2.

Page 114 Referred to in Ed Creagh's column, *The Sumter Daily Item* (Sumter, S.C.), Sept. 17, 1957.

Page 116 Wm. H. Russell: *My Diary North and South* (Boston, 1863), p. 180.

Page 121 Ulrich B. Phillips: *American Negro Slavery* (New York, 1918), p. 290.

Page 122 Clement Eaton: *A History of the Old South* (New York, 1949), p. 371.

Page 125 Mrs. M. L. Avary: *Dixie after the War* (Boston, 1937), p. 314.

Page 141 Frances Anne Kemble: *Journal of a Residence on a Georgian Plantation* (New York, 1863), p. 139.

Page 166 Robert Penn Warren: *Segregation* (New York, 1956), p. 15.

Page 171 Kemble: op. cit., p. 56.

Page 173 Frederick L. Olmsted: *A Journey in the Back Country* (New York, 1860), p. 64.

Page 182 William Archer: *Through Afro-American* (London, 1910), pp. 102–3.

Page 193 Reported in *Southern School News*, December 1956 (Vol. III, no. 3), p. 10.

Page 194 Walter Hines Page: "Rebuilding of Old Commonwealths," *Atlantic Monthly*, May 1902, p. 652.

Page 209 Captain Basil Hall: *Travels in North America in the Years 1827 & 1828* (Philadelphia, 1829), Vol. II, p. 239.
Broadus Mitchell: *William Gregg, Factory Master of the Old South* (Chapel Hill, 1928), p. 20.

Page 214 Ben Robertson: *Red Hills and Cotton* (New York, 1942), p. 246.

Page 217 Edgar Gardner Murphy: *The Basis of Ascendancy* (New York, 1909), p. 47.

Page 218 Reported in *Southern School News*, September 1950 (Vol. III, no. 3), p. 10.

Page 225 Sir Charles Lyell: *Travels in North America in the Years 1841–2* (New York, 1909), Vol. II, p. 52.

Page 226 Simkins: op. cit., p. 42.

Page 227 Eaton: op. cit., p. 85.

Page 228 Lyell: op. cit., Vol. II, p. 86.

Page 230 Murphy: op. cit., pp. 15–16.

Page 237 In report of Carl Schurz, in *Executive Documents of the Senate . . . First Session, Thirty-Ninth Congress*, Vol. I, no. 2, p. 2.

Page 238 Major John DeForest: *A Union Officer in the Reconstruction* (New Haven, 1948), p. 155.

Page 240 Kemble: op. cit., p. 125.

Page 243 F. L. Olmsted: *Journey in the Seaboard Slave States* (New York, 1904), Vol. I, p. 205.

Page 246 Kemble: op. cit., p. 67.

Page 248 Alexis de Tocqueville: *Democracy in America* (New York, 1945), Vol. I, p. 373.

Page 249 Katherine Lumpkin: *The Making of a Southerner* (New York, 1947), pp. 133–4.

Page 252 Reported in *Southern School News*, June 1957 (Vol. III, no. 12), p. 13.

Page 253 Reported in *Southern School News*, July 1955 (Vol. II, no. 1), p. 16.

Page 262 John T. Trowbridge: *The Desolate South, 1865–1866*, edited by Gordon Carroll (New York, 1956), p. 197.

Page 264 *The Private Journal of William Henry Ravenel, 1859–1877*, edited by A. R. Childs (Columbia, S.C., 1947), p. 301.

INDEX

A Note on the Author

JAMES MCBRIDE DABBS lives in Mayesville, South Carolina, where he was born in 1896. He received his A.B. from the University of South Carolina in 1916, his M.A. from Clark University in 1917, and was a second and then a first lieutenant in the Field Artillery during World War I (1917–1919). After the Armistice he returned to Mayesville to farm for his father, but in 1921 he left the plantation to teach college English and do further graduate work. In 1930 he started writing free-lance articles for magazines, and in 1937, abandoned a university career to devote himself full-time to his plantation and to writing. Although Mr. Dabbs has had almost one hundred articles published in magazines all over the country, *The Southern Heritage* is his first book. In 1957 he was elected president of the Southern Regional Council. He is a member of the board of directors of the Penn Community Services in Beaufort, S.C., an Elder in the Presbyterian Church in the United States, and a member of the executive committee of the Fellowship of Southern Churchmen.

A NOTE ON THE TYPE

The text of this book was set on the Linotype in JANSON, a recutting made direct from the type cast from matrices made by Anton Janson. Whether or not Janson was of Dutch ancestry is not known, but it is known that he purchased a foundry and was a practicing type-founder in Leipzig during the years 1600 to 1687. Janson's first specimen sheet was issued in 1675. His successor issued a specimen sheet showing all of the Janson types in 1689.

His type is an excellent example of the influential and sturdy Dutch types that prevailed in England prior to the development by William Caslon of his own incomparable designs, which he evolved from these Dutch faces. The Dutch in their turn had been influenced by Garamond in France. The general tone of Janson, however, is darker than Garamond and has a sturdiness and substance quite different from its predecessors. It is a highly legible type, and its individual letters have a pleasing variety of design. Its heavy and light strokes make it sharp and clear, and the full-page effect is characterful and harmonious.

This book was composed, printed, and bound by KINGSPORT PRESS, INC., Kingsport, Tennessee. Paper manufactured by P. H. GLATFELTER COMPANY, Spring Grove, Pennsylvania. Designed by CARL HERTZOG.